THE
BIG SMALL
PLASTIC
PROBLEM

AN ECO-FRIENDLY GUIDE
TO MICROPLASTICS, WASTE REDUCTION,
AND CREATIVE RECYCLING PROJECTS
FOR KIDS AND ADULTS

Wonder Full Books

Illustrations and Artwork by
Minimal Blue, Brian Goff, Yuliya Pauliukevich,Matt Cole,
Chanwit Yasamut and Giuseppe Ramos

Wonder Full Books
First edition 2025

Also available in eBook.

ISBN: 9798267714686

CONTENTS

PART 1 – THE PLASTIC STORY 9

CHAPTER 1: A FANTASTIC INVENTION 11
FROM BAKELITE TO BARBIE DOLLS: HOW PLASTIC
REVOLUTIONISED THE WORLD 12
WHY PLASTIC WAS SEEN AS MIRACULOUS 14
THE MIRACLE MATERIAL... 16
FROM MARVEL TO MOUNTAINS OF IT.............................. 17
CAMPING WITHOUT PLASTIC 18

CHAPTER 2: THE AGE OF DISPOSABLE EVERYTHING 20
THE POST-WWII BOOM AND THE BIRTH OF THE THROWAWAY
SOCIETY 21
A FUN TIMELINE OF ICONIC PLASTIC INVENTIONS 22
QUIRKY PLASTIC FACTS: FROM SPACE TO THE CATWALK 26
PLASTIC IN SPACE 26
PLASTIC IN FASHION 27
PLASTIC AS POP ART 28
BUBBLE WRAP AND BEYOND 29

PART 2 – TINY PLASTICS, HUGE PROBLEM 30

CHAPTER 3: WHAT ARE MICROPLASTICS? 32
EXPLAINED FOR KIDS & ADULTS 32
THE COOKIE THAT NEVER GETS EATEN 34
WHERE MICROPLASTICS HIDE 35

CHAPTER 4: PLASTIC IN WEIRD PLACES 39
MICROPLASTICS IN RAINCLOUDS, ARCTIC SNOW, AND HUMAN
LUNGS 39
CLOSING THOUGHT 45

CHAPTER 5: ANIMALS VS. PLASTIC 46
SEA TURTLES MISTAKING BAGS FOR JELLYFISH 47
BIRDS WITH PLASTIC BELLIES 48
INSECTS AND WORMS CARRYING MICROPLASTICS INTO SOIL 50

CHAPTER 6: US VS. PLASTIC 53
MICROPLASTICS IN BLOOD, BREAST MILK, AND BEER 54
POSSIBLE HEALTH RISKS OF MICROPLASTICS 56
A BALANCED VIEW 59
SPOT THE SNEAKY PLASTIC 59

PART 3 – WHAT THE WORLD IS DOING 62

CHAPTER 7: THE FIGHT AGAINST PLASTIC 64
MICROBEAD BANS AND BAG CHARGES 64
GLOBAL PROJECTS AND GOVERNMENT BANS 67
THE WILD FUTURE: PLASTIC-EATING BACTERIA AND
MUSHROOMS 69
A NOTE OF CAUTION 72

CHAPTER 8: IS IT ENOUGH? 73
IS IT ENOUGH? THE HONEST BUT HOPEFUL TRUTH 74
THE BALANCING ACT 75
HUMANS VS. PLASTIC: WHO'S WINNING? 76

PART 4 – WHAT YOU CAN DO 79

CHAPTER 9: PLASTIC-FREE SWAPS 81
HOUSEHOLD HACKS FOR A PLASTIC-LIGHTER LIFE 81
DONNY WONDER'S PLASTIC SWAP BINGO...................... 86

CHAPTER 10: FAMILY PLASTIC DETECTIVE.................... 89
HOW TO DO A HOUSEHOLD PLASTIC AUDIT 90
TURN IT INTO A GAME: SPOTTING SNEAKY PLASTIC 93
WHY IT WORKS... 96

CHAPTER 11: LIVING THE PLASTIC-LIGHT LIFE.............. 97
EASY THINGS WITH BIG IMPACT 98
OTHER EASY WINS TO ADD TO YOUR TOOLKIT 100
THE BOTTOM LINE 101
SURVIVE A WEEKEND WITHOUT SINGLE-USE PLASTIC 101
WHY THIS MATTERS 102

PART 5 – FUN WITH RECYCLING 104

CHAPTER 12: ARTS & CRAFTS INDOORS 106
BOTTLE CAP MOSAICS...107
MILK JUG HELMETS & MASKS 109
PLASTIC BOTTLE LANTERNS 111
WONDER FULL CRAFT CHALLENGES 114
WHY DO THESE CHALLENGES?....................................116

CHAPTER 13: GREEN GARDEN PROJECTS................... 117
BOTTLE-BUILT GREENHOUSES 118
DIY PLANT POTS.. 121
A SCARECROW MADE OF ODDS & ENDS (WITH A DONNY
WONDER HAT) 125

CHAPTER 14: THE BIG PLASTIC FINALE..................... 128
PLASTICS: USEFUL BUT DANGEROUS............................ 129
WE CAN'T DO EVERYTHING, BUT WE CAN DO SOMETHING 130
WHY SMALL ACTIONS MATTER 130
PICK YOUR BATTLES 131
WHAT YOU CAN'T CONTROL 132
THE BIGGER PICTURE.. 132

CLOSING WORDS OF ENCOURAGEMENT 133

MORE FROM
WONDER FULL BOOKS

A Wonderfully Weird Would You Rather!?! Book
for Kids Ages 7–12 and Probably Teens

Indoor Rainy Day Activities
for Kids and Teens (Illustrated)

Summer Activities for Kids 9-12 (Illustrated)
100 Fun Outdoor Games for Boys and Girls

PART 1
THE
PLASTIC STORY

Before we talk about the tiny troublemakers known as **microplastics**, we need to rewind the tape and look at where it all began. Plastic didn't just show up one day in the form of crisp packets, Lego bricks, and shopping bags. It started as a marvel — a shiny new material that seemed to solve all kinds of problems.

Imagine a world before plastic: no lightweight containers, no waterproof jackets, no cheap toys, no cling film keeping your sandwiches fresh. The first plastics, like **Bakelite**, were hailed as miracles. They were tough, flexible, and could be shaped into almost anything. Suddenly, we could make products faster, cheaper, and more colourful than ever before. The future looked plastic — and people loved it.

But, as with many "miracle" inventions, the story soon took a twist. Plastic became too good, too cheap, and far too disposable. By the mid-20th century, we weren't just using plastic — we were **drowning in it**.

From Barbie dolls to bubble wrap, Tupperware to takeaway cups, plastic leapt into every corner of our lives. And once society got hooked, there was no turning back.

This part of the book is your backstage pass to the **rise of plastic**. We'll uncover how it went from a clever invention to a cultural juggernaut, reshaping everything from fashion to food storage, from space exploration to Saturday morning toy boxes.

And of course, Donny Wonder has a thought to kick us off:

"Try going camping without plastic pegs, waterproofs, or your trusty Thermos. Yeah, good luck with that. You'd be wetter than a sea sponge in a rainstorm."

So grab your metaphorical hard hat, because we're about to step into the factory where it all began: **the birth of plastic.**

CHAPTER 1:
A FANTASTIC INVENTION

Let's roll back to the early 1900s, when the world was buzzing with invention. Cars were clattering down streets, the first aeroplanes were wobbling through the sky, and scientists were hunting for new materials that could outdo wood, glass, and metal. Enter **plastic** — the wonder-stuff that would change everything.

The first superstar of the plastic family was **Bakelite**, invented in 1907. Tough, heat-resistant, and cheap, it was soon everywhere: in radios, telephones, jewellery, even buttons on your grandad's coat. For the first time, humans had created a material that didn't just imitate nature — it outperformed it.

And people went wild for it. Suddenly, manufacturers could mould and mass-produce products faster and cheaper than ever before. No more expensive ivory combs or fragile glass insulators — plastic could do the job better, lighter, and brighter. By the time the mid-century rolled around, it was shaping everything from Barbie dolls to car dashboards.

Why did plastic seem so miraculous? Because it ticked all the boxes. It was **cheap, flexible, durable, and colourful.** It didn't rust, it didn't shatter, and it could be bent into just about any shape you fancied. To the world at large, it felt like science had handed humanity a golden ticket.

And here's Donny Wonder's take:

> *"Imagine trying to go camping without plastic*
> *pegs, waterproofs, or your trusty Thermos!*
> *You'd end up with soggy sandwiches, a collapsed tent,*
> *and socks so wet they could host tadpoles."*

So yes, plastic began as a genuine marvel — a material that seemed to unlock a future of endless possibilities. But, as we'll see, that fantastic invention came with consequences nobody saw coming.

FROM BAKELITE TO BARBIE DOLLS: HOW PLASTIC REVOLUTIONISED THE WORLD

When Belgian chemist **Leo Baekeland** cooked up a new synthetic material in 1907, he couldn't have known he was about to flip human history upside down. His invention, called **Bakelite**, was the world's first true plastic — a tough, heat-resistant resin that refused to bend to the old rules of nature. Unlike wood, it wouldn't rot. Unlike glass, it wouldn't shatter. Unlike metal, it wouldn't rust. It was cheap to make, easy to mould, and strong enough to take a beating.

Within years, Bakelite was popping up everywhere. It coated electrical wires, shaped into radios and telephones, and gleamed from the jewellery boxes of fashionable ladies in the Roaring Twenties. It was called "the material of a thousand uses," and for good reason: if you could dream it, Bakelite could probably be moulded into it.

That was just the start. As the decades rolled on, new forms of plastic joined the party. Nylon stockings gave women a stylish (and durable) wardrobe upgrade in the 1930s. During World War II, plastics played a crucial role in replacing scarce materials like rubber and metal, finding their way into everything from aircraft parts to parachutes. Suddenly, plastic wasn't just a handy alternative — it was essential.

By the 1950s, the post-war boom gave plastics a starring role in daily life. Imagine stepping into a typical living room of the era: Tupperware tubs stacked in the kitchen, colourful melamine plates on the dinner table, vinyl records spinning on the turntable. Plastics weren't just practical — they were modern, fashionable, and fun.

And then came the **Barbie doll** in 1959, a symbol of both the glamour and mass-production power of plastic. Sleek, shiny, and nearly indestructible, Barbie became a cultural icon and sold by the millions. She was lightweight, affordable, and could be dressed in endless outfits, all thanks to plastic. From that moment on, plastic wasn't just part of our homes — it shaped childhoods, culture, and imagination.

The revolution was unstoppable. Lego bricks (patented in 1958) gave children colourful worlds to build. Plastic packaging transformed shopping, keeping food fresher for longer and cutting down on waste — or so people thought. And disposable items, from razors to pens to cameras, made convenience king. Plastic was no longer just a material; it was the very symbol of modern living.

It's easy to see why people fell in love with it. Plastic was a miracle worker: lightweight, flexible, durable, colourful, and cheap. It could mimic expensive materials like ivory, jade, and tortoiseshell, making luxury affordable to ordinary people. It gave designers and inventors new freedom to create shapes, colours, and gadgets that were once impossible.

But miracles often come with fine print. At the time, nobody stopped to ask: *what happens when all this plastic reaches the end of its useful life?*

And here's Donny Wonder's cheeky thought for the road:

"If Bakelite was the granddad of plastics, Barbie was its first pop star. Just imagine: the world went from clunky telephones to dolls with perfect hair, all in a few decades. If that's not revolutionary, I don't know what is."

WHY PLASTIC WAS SEEN AS MIRACULOUS

When plastic first appeared on the scene, it must have felt like science fiction come to life. Here was a material that could do things wood, metal, and glass could only dream of. To manufacturers, designers, and ordinary families, plastic looked less like a product and more like a superpower.

- **Cheap**

Before plastics, many household goods were made from natural materials like ivory, bone, tortoiseshell, or wood. They were expensive, limited, and sometimes cruelly sourced (the elephant population would nod in agreement here). Plastic changed the game. Suddenly, you could make thousands of combs, buttons, or toys for a fraction of the price.

Cheapness meant **accessibility**. Families who could never afford fancy ornaments, shiny jewellery, or durable containers suddenly found their homes filled with bright, modern goods. From Bakelite radios to colourful melamine plates, plastic gave ordinary people a slice of luxury.

- **Flexible**

Wood snaps. Glass shatters. Metal bends, dents, or rusts. But plastic? Plastic could be anything you wanted it to be. It could bend without breaking, stretch without tearing, and mould into shapes that were once unthinkable.

This flexibility fuelled creativity. Inventors and designers weren't limited by nature anymore. They could design chairs with wild curves, bottles that squeezed, and toys with moving parts. Plastic could imitate other materials or become something entirely new. It was like clay, only far stronger and longer-lasting.

- **Durable**

And here's the kicker: plastic doesn't rot. It doesn't rust. It doesn't crumble away in the rain. Drop it, and it bounces. Leave it outside, and it soldiers on. Compared to fragile glass or heavy metal, plastic was a tank disguised as a feather.

This durability felt like a blessing. A toy wouldn't break after one rough play session. A picnic set could survive countless summer outings. A plastic bag could be used again and again without tearing. To a world still recovering from the rationing and scarcity of World War II, a tough, reliable material was nothing short of miraculous.

THE MIRACLE MATERIAL

Put those qualities together — cheap, flexible, durable — and you had a recipe for revolution. Plastic wasn't just a new option; it was the answer to problems people didn't even realise they had. It made products more affordable, designs more daring, and lifestyles more convenient.

Of course, the irony is that these same "miraculous" qualities are what make plastic such a nightmare today. It's so durable it sticks around for centuries. It's so cheap we treat it as disposable. And it's so flexible it sneaks into every corner of our lives, from food packaging to clothing fibres.

But at the time, it wasn't seen as a problem. It was seen as progress. Plastic was the future, and the future looked shiny.

And here's Donny Wonder's cheeky take:

> *"Durable? Let me tell you — I've got a plastic lunchbox from the 1980s that's survived more camping trips than my knees. If cockroaches inherit the earth, that lunchbox will be right there beside them."*

FROM MARVEL TO MOUNTAINS OF IT

By the mid-20th century, plastic had proven itself. It was the material of modern life — cheap, flexible, durable, and practically unstoppable. Radios, telephones, toys, kitchenware, cars, clothing, packaging… plastic was everywhere, and people couldn't get enough of it.

But here's the twist: what started as a miracle slowly turned into a monster. Because when something is *that* cheap and *that* durable, people stop treating it like a treasure. Instead, they treat it like it's endless and disposable.

That's exactly what happened after World War II. Factories that once churned out war supplies turned their machines toward household goods. Supermarkets embraced plastic packaging. Food came wrapped, drinks came bottled, and gadgets came sealed in shiny new skins of plastic.

The miracle material of yesterday became the **throwaway culture of tomorrow.**

Or, as Donny Wonder puts it:

> *"Plastic went from 'Look at this amazing thing that will last forever!' to 'Meh, just chuck it — we'll make another.' Somewhere along the line, the world swapped wonder for waste."*

CAMPING WITHOUT PLASTIC

Alright, let's play a game of imagination. Picture this: you're heading out for a weekend of camping, the birds are singing, the tent's strapped to your back, and you're feeling like a rugged outdoor legend. Only one catch — no plastic allowed.

First problem? **Tent pegs.** Forget those neat little plastic-topped spikes. You'd be hammering whittled twigs into the ground, and trust me, they don't hold when the wind picks up. Say goodbye to your shelter — and hello to a night under soggy clouds.

Second problem? **Waterproofs.** Without plastic-based fabrics, your "raincoat" is basically a woolly jumper. Which, in British weather, is the fast track to hypothermia. You'd be wetter than a haddock's handshake.

Third problem? **The Thermos flask.** That humble plastic-sealed marvel that keeps tea hot for hours? Gone. Instead, you're sipping lukewarm river water out of a tin mug, muttering about how civilisation went wrong.

And don't even get me started on **torches without plastic casings**, or trying to haul your gear in a canvas sack that leaks like a colander.

So yes — plastic might be today's environmental headache, but there's no denying it made life in the great outdoors a whole lot easier.

"Imagine trying to go camping without plastic pegs, waterproofs, or your trusty Thermos! You'd return home not with memories, but pneumonia."

CHAPTER 2
THE AGE OF
DISPOSABLE EVERYTHING

When the guns of World War II finally fell silent, a new sound took over: the cheerful burp of Tupperware lids, the snap of Lego bricks, and the rustle of plastic packaging. Factories that once produced parachutes and helmets now churned out toys, containers, and kitchen gadgets. Plastic had marched off the battlefield and into the living room.

The world was rebuilding, families were growing, and people wanted convenience. Plastic delivered it in spades. Lightweight, colourful, and—most dangerously—cheap, it became the cornerstone of a new way of living: the **throwaway society.** Why wash when you could toss? Why fix when you could replace?

In this chapter, we'll explore how plastic went from miracle invention to cultural phenomenon. We'll trace the post-war boom, peek at a timeline of iconic inventions (from Barbie dolls to bubble wrap), and even uncover a few quirky places plastic turned up—like in outer space and on the catwalk.

> *"We didn't just embrace plastic after the war—*
> *we hugged it so tight that half a century later*
> *we're still trying to peel it off."*

THE POST-WWII BOOM AND THE BIRTH OF THE THROWAWAY SOCIETY

When World War II ended in 1945, the world was tired of ration books, shortages, and mending the same worn-out jumper for the fifth winter in a row. People wanted shiny new things, and they wanted them fast. Factories that had been churning out parachutes, helmets, and weapons suddenly had spare capacity — and a new mission: make life easier, brighter, and more modern.

Enter plastic.

Plastics had proved their worth during the war — nylon parachutes saved lives, lightweight aircraft parts boosted performance, and plasticised fabrics kept soldiers (mostly) dry. So when peace arrived, manufacturers turned those same materials toward peacetime living. Cheap, lightweight, and easy to mass-produce, plastic was perfect for the booming consumer culture of the 1950s.

Suddenly, kitchens filled with colourful **Tupperware** that promised to keep food fresh forever (and hosted whole parties to show it off). Dining tables swapped heavy china for bright **melamine plates** that wouldn't shatter if dropped. Supermarkets wrapped food in plastic film that looked clean and modern. Even nappies and razors went from washable to disposable — a miracle for busy parents, a nightmare for future landfills.

This shift wasn't just about products. It was about **mindset**. Plastic taught people that it was okay to throw things away. Why bother scrubbing greasy cutlery when you could toss it in the bin? Why patch up an old toy when a new one cost pennies? The message was clear: convenience had won, and durability was now less about keeping an item forever and more about making sure it lasted just long enough to be used once.

The phrase "**throwaway society**" was born in the 1950s, and for good reason. Everything seemed designed to be temporary — plates, cups, bags, bottles, even fashion. Plastic wasn't just a material anymore; it was a lifestyle, one that promised endless newness without the fuss of looking after what you already had.

> *"Imagine the marketing pitch: 'Here's a brand-new material that will last forever! And the best part? You only use it once before chucking it in the bin!' Somewhere, common sense took an early retirement."*

A FUN TIMELINE OF ICONIC PLASTIC INVENTIONS

Plastics didn't just sneak quietly into our homes after the war — they burst through the front door with colour, convenience, and more than a few party tricks. Let's take a walk through some of the plastic pioneers that defined the mid-20th century and beyond.

1946
THE TUPPERWARE TAKEOVER

Earl Tupper (yes, he was a real person) invented an airtight plastic container with a lid that "burped" when sealed. It kept food fresher for longer, and soon kitchens everywhere were stacked with them. But the real genius wasn't just the container — it was the *Tupperware Party*.

In the 1950s, housewives across America hosted living-room sales events where neighbours gathered to gossip, snack, and watch the miraculous burping lid in action. Plastic wasn't just practical anymore — it was *social*. By the end of the decade, Tupperware had gone global, and the humble food container became a symbol of modern domestic life.

> *"Never underestimate the power of a burping lid to bring people together. Forget Zoom calls — if we'd stuck with Tupperware parties, we'd have solved loneliness decades ago."*

1958
LEGO: THE BRICK THAT BUILT IMAGINATION

In Denmark, toy maker Ole Kirk Christiansen patented the interlocking plastic brick we now know as **Lego**. Unlike wooden blocks that toppled easily, Lego's clever stud-and-tube design meant creations could be stacked, snapped apart, and rebuilt endlessly.

Lego gave children a universe of possibility in a box —
castles, spaceships, cities, or whatever their imaginations
dreamed up. It was colourful, reusable, and nearly
indestructible (though alarmingly effective at crippling
bare feet at 3 a.m.).

More than just a toy, Lego became a cultural phenomenon.
By the 21st century, there were Lego movies, Lego theme
parks, and even Lego recreations of the Taj Mahal. And it
all started with a plastic brick that clicked.

*"Step on one Lego brick in the dark,
and you'll discover new curse words in
languages you didn't even know you spoke."*

1959
BARBIE: PLASTIC GLAMOUR
IN MINIATURE

When Ruth Handler introduced the **Barbie doll**, she wasn't
just selling a toy — she was selling a dream. Injection-
moulded plastic gave Barbie her sleek form, shiny hair, and
endless wardrobe options. She was glamorous,
aspirational, and controversial all at once.

Barbie revolutionised the toy industry, becoming both a
beloved playmate and a lightning rod for cultural debates.
Whether you see her as a feminist icon or a fashion fantasy,
there's no denying she owes her existence to the miracle
of plastic.

1960
BUBBLE WRAP:
POPPING INTO HISTORY

Believe it or not, bubble wrap wasn't invented for packaging at all. Engineers Alfred Fielding and Marc Chavannes originally created it as a new kind of textured wallpaper. The wallpaper idea bombed, but they quickly realised the bubbles made perfect shock absorbers for shipping fragile goods.

Bubble wrap became a packaging staple — but let's be honest, its real contribution to humanity is stress relief. There's something universally satisfying about popping bubble after bubble, one thumb press at a time. Today, it's as much a toy as a protective layer.

> *"Somewhere out there, an entire factory produces bubble wrap just so the rest of us can pop it for fun. If that isn't proof of civilisation's priorities, I don't know what is."*

1970S ONWARDS
PLASTIC EVERYWHERE

By the 1970s, plastic inventions came thick and fast. **PET bottles** made soft drinks cheap and portable. **Vinyl records** gave music lovers hours of tunes. **Cassette tapes and CDs** brought entire albums into your pocket. Polyester clothes filled wardrobes, and plastic bags filled shopping trolleys.

Plastics weren't just products anymore — they were culture, convenience, and sometimes even luxury. They changed how we ate, played, dressed, travelled, and even how we relaxed.

*

By the time the 1980s rolled around, plastic had truly conquered the modern world. From toys to fashion to packaging, it had embedded itself into daily life so completely that nobody could imagine living without it. And more importantly, nobody *wanted* to.

QUIRKY PLASTIC FACTS: FROM SPACE TO THE CATWALK

By the 1960s, plastic wasn't just filling cupboards and toy chests — it was shooting for the stars and strutting down fashion runways. It had truly gone from household helper to cultural icon. Here are some of the strangest and most fascinating ways plastic showed off its versatility.

PLASTIC IN SPACE

When humans set their sights on the stars, plastic came along for the ride. The Apollo missions of the 1960s and '70s relied on plastics for insulation, seals, and lightweight equipment. Astronaut suits used multiple layers of plastic-based fabrics to keep out deadly radiation and extreme temperatures, all while letting astronauts bend and move. Without it, Neil Armstrong would've stepped onto the Moon looking like a frozen popsicle.

Even spacecraft interiors relied on plastic. From protective coatings to food packaging, plastic kept things light, safe, and sterile. To this day, every rocket launched into orbit carries a hefty dose of polymers — proof that the "miracle material" wasn't just down-to-earth.

> *"Forget Tang and dehydrated ice cream —*
> *the real unsung hero of space travel is plastic.*
> *Without it, astronauts wouldn't be bouncing on*
> *the Moon; they'd be cryogenically stored there."*

PLASTIC IN FASHION

If you've ever looked back at old family photos and wondered why everyone in the 1970s looked like they were wrapped in a shiny crisp packet, you can thank plastic. **Polyester, nylon, and PVC** became staples of wardrobes, promising durability and easy washing. No more ironing mountains of cotton shirts — polyester didn't crease (much).

Designers embraced plastic with a futuristic flair. In the 1960s, fashion icon André Courrèges sent models down the runway in white PVC boots and vinyl dresses that looked like they belonged on a spaceship. Plastic was seen as sleek, modern, and space-age cool.

Of course, it wasn't all glamour. Polyester trousers trapped sweat like a sauna, and PVC dresses didn't breathe. But style often trumps comfort, and for a while, plastic fashion was the height of trendiness.

> *"They say fashion comes at a price.*
> *In the '70s, that price was smelling like you'd*
> *run a marathon just by standing still*
> *in polyester trousers."*

PLASTIC AS POP ART

Even artists couldn't resist plastic's allure. In the 1960s, Andy Warhol and the Pop Art movement embraced plastic culture, celebrating the artificial, the colourful, and the disposable. Warhol's **Campbell's Soup Cans** weren't made of plastic, but they captured the spirit of consumerism plastic embodied. Meanwhile, sculptors experimented with acrylics and resins, bending and moulding them into wild new forms.

Plastic wasn't just practical anymore — it was symbolic. It represented the modern world: bright, bold, and a little bit fake.

*

By the time the 1980s rolled in, plastic had conquered not just kitchens and toy boxes but also outer space, fashion magazines, and art galleries. It wasn't just a material — it was a **movement.** Plastic wasn't hiding in the background anymore. It was centre stage.

And yet, as society embraced it, one question went largely unasked: *what happens when all this plastic outlives us?*

That's where the story of plastic begins to twist again — from fashion statement to environmental burden.

BUBBLE WRAP AND BEYOND

I sometimes wonder if the real reason humanity embraced plastic wasn't Tupperware or Barbie, but **bubble wrap.** Forget its usefulness in packaging fragile goods — the joy of popping those little air pockets is reason enough to crown it mankind's greatest invention.

Imagine a world without it. Every time a fragile parcel arrived, you'd just open the box and... nothing. No stress relief, no satisfying *pop-pop-pop*, just boring old crumpled paper. I reckon half the world's collective frustration would've gone nuclear by now without bubble wrap to calm us down.

And fashion? Don't get me started. I once wore a polyester shirt on a hot summer's day. By lunchtime, I smelled like a compost heap wrapped in clingfilm. Glamorous? Not even close. Durable? Oh, definitely — that shirt is still lurking in my wardrobe, indestructible as ever, waiting to haunt me.

> *"Bubble wrap kept our parcels safe,*
> *but polyester nearly finished us off. Call it a draw."*

PART 2

TINY PLASTICS, HUGE PROBLEM

Plastic bottles, Barbie dolls, and bubble wrap are easy enough to spot. They're big, colourful, and (if you trip over Lego at 3 a.m.) painful reminders of just how much plastic has taken over our lives. But what happens when those big plastic things break down into pieces so small you can't even see them?

Welcome to the strange, unsettling world of **microplastics.**

These tiny fragments are everywhere. They're in the clothes we wear, the food we eat, the water we drink, and even the air we breathe. They might be smaller than a sesame seed, but their impact is enormous. Scientists are finding them in places that sound like the set of a science fiction film — Arctic snow, rainclouds drifting over cities, the bellies of birds, and even inside human bloodstreams.

This part of the book takes you on a tour of the invisible problem we can't escape. We'll break it down so both kids and adults can get their heads around it: what microplastics are, how they travel, where they hide, and why animals (and we humans) keep ending up as unwilling plastic storage units.

But don't worry — Donny Wonder is here to make sure it's not all doom and gloom. Expect fun metaphors, weird discoveries, and a dare or two along the way.

> *"Think of microplastics like the crumbs from a cookie that never gets eaten. Except this cookie isn't chocolate chip — it's everywhere, it's eternal, and it's not nearly as tasty."*

So, let's zoom in on the problem. Because sometimes, the smallest pieces cause the biggest headaches.

CHAPTER 3
WHAT ARE MICROPLASTICS?

We've seen how plastic took over the world in big, bold, colourful ways — from Lego bricks to bubble wrap. But now it's time to zoom in. Way in. Because the real problem with plastic isn't just the bottles on the beach or the bags tangled in trees. It's the tiny fragments you can't even see.

These are **microplastics** — pieces so small they slip into water, air, soil, animals, and even us. They might look harmless, but they're everywhere, and they never go away.

In this chapter, we'll break it down (pun intended). We'll explain what microplastics are, use some fun metaphors to make sense of them, and reveal the sneaky places they hide. By the end, you'll realise the tiniest plastics are the biggest troublemakers of all.

> *"Think of them as the invisible sprinkles nobody asked for — scattered across the entire planet, and stuck to everything forever."*

EXPLAINED FOR KIDS & ADULTS

Imagine snapping a chocolate bar in half. Crumbs scatter everywhere, too small to pick up, but you know they're there.

Now replace the chocolate with plastic — a water bottle, a shopping bag, a toy — and imagine it breaking down into tinier and tinier crumbs over time. Those crumbs don't melt, dissolve, or vanish. They just keep breaking down, becoming smaller and smaller until you can barely see them. That's the world of **microplastics.**

Scientists define microplastics as pieces of plastic less than **5 millimetres long** — about the size of a sesame seed or smaller. Some are so tiny you'd need a microscope to spot them. But no matter how small they get, one thing never changes: plastic doesn't disappear. It lingers.

For kids, think of it this way: if you drop a biscuit in the garden, ants will find it, nibble it, and eventually it's gone. Drop a plastic wrapper instead, and it doesn't go away. It just crumbles into smaller and smaller pieces, hiding in the soil, blowing in the wind, or washing into rivers. Nature can eat biscuits, but it can't eat plastic.

For adults, here's the blunt truth: plastics are designed to last. That's what made them so miraculous in the first place. But that same durability means they outlive us, our kids, and probably our grandkids too. Instead of rotting or rusting, plastics break into microscopic pieces that slip into the food chain, the water cycle, and even the air we breathe.

> *"Plastic is like the party guest who never leaves. First, they're big and obvious. Then they shrink into the background. But they're still there — forever — eating your snacks and hogging your sofa."*

THE COOKIE THAT
NEVER GETS EATEN

Sometimes, the easiest way to understand something complicated is with a good metaphor. So let's talk cookies.

Picture your favourite cookie — let's say chocolate chip. Now imagine dropping it on the floor and smashing it into a hundred pieces. Those pieces are easy enough to see and sweep up. But if you kept crumbling the cookie into smaller and smaller bits, soon you'd have tiny crumbs stuck in the carpet, floating in the air, and hiding in the cracks of the floorboards. You could hoover all day, and you'd *still* never get every crumb.

That's what happens to plastic. A bottle doesn't just vanish when it's tossed aside. Sunlight, wind, and waves break it down into smaller and smaller pieces — but it never fully disappears. The crumbs of the "plastic cookie" just keep scattering, spreading, and sneaking into places you'd never expect.

Now here's the scary part: unlike cookie crumbs, nothing in nature comes along to clean them up. Ants won't carry them off. Rain won't wash them away. They just sit there. Forever. Scientists estimate that every piece of plastic ever made still exists in some form — maybe a Lego brick in someone's attic, maybe fibres floating in the sea, maybe microscopic specks drifting in the air you're breathing right now.

For kids, think of it like glitter. Spill a bit, and suddenly it's *everywhere* — on your clothes, in your hair, stuck to the dog, still turning up months later. That's microplastics. Except glitter might be annoying, while microplastics are much more serious.

For adults, think of it like dust. No matter how often you clean, it comes back. Only instead of skin cells or pollen, this dust is made of indestructible plastic that's weaving itself into the fabric of the natural world.

> *"The plastic cookie crumbles, but nobody ever eats it. Instead, the crumbs keep piling up until you find one in your tea, one in your socks, and one probably lodged in your left nostril. Bon appétit."*

WHERE MICROPLASTICS HIDE

Microplastics don't just appear out of nowhere. They sneak into the world from some very ordinary, very everyday places — often right under our noses. You don't have to be standing on a polluted beach or next to a landfill to be surrounded by them. Chances are, they're in your house right now. Let's meet the main culprits.

CLOTHES FIBRES

That comfy fleece you love? Or the stretchy sports top that keeps you cool? Chances are, they're made of synthetic fabrics like polyester, nylon, or acrylic — all types of plastic.

Every time you wash them, thousands of tiny fibres shed and escape down the drain. They're too small to be caught by most washing machine filters, so they head straight into rivers and oceans.

To put it into perspective, a single load of laundry can release up to **700,000 plastic fibres.** That's like turning your washing machine into a confetti cannon aimed at the planet.

"So technically, every time you do the laundry, you're hosting a microplastic party. And the fish are the unlucky guests."

PACKAGING

Plastic packaging is everywhere. Crisp packets, cling film, takeaway containers — they all shed tiny fragments as they're made, used, and thrown away. Even when you carefully recycle or toss them in the bin, the journey doesn't stop there. Packaging breaks apart in landfills, or flakes off as it's handled, sneaking into soil, water, and air.

And here's the kicker: some microplastics don't even need to *break down*. They're already manufactured small — like the infamous **microbeads** once found in face scrubs and toothpaste. Governments have banned many of them now, but the legacy of those "scrubbing bubbles" is still washing around out there.

CAR TYRES

Yes, even your car is a microplastic factory on wheels. Tyres aren't just made of rubber; they contain a hefty dose of plastic polymers. Every time you drive, the friction of rubber on road shaves off tiny particles — and there are billions of cars in the world doing this every day.

These tyre shavings don't just vanish. They wash into drains when it rains, get blown into the air by passing traffic, and settle into soil and waterways. In some cities, **tyre wear is one of the largest single sources of microplastics**. So every trip to the shops leaves behind a plastic footprint we don't see.

"Forget exhaust fumes —
your tyres are basically leaving
a breadcrumb trail of microplastics
across the planet.

Hansel and Gretel had nothing on us."

*

From laundry rooms to motorways, microplastics are constantly being released by the way we live. They're invisible hitchhikers, clinging to our daily habits and scattering themselves far and wide. And as we'll soon see, they don't just hang around in obvious places — they travel into some of the weirdest corners of the planet.

CHAPTER 4
PLASTIC IN WEIRD PLACES

It's one thing to find microplastics in your fleece jacket or a bag of crisps. That makes sense — they came from there in the first place. But scientists keep discovering them in places so strange, it feels like the start of a sci-fi novel.

Snow in the Arctic. Clouds drifting above busy cities. Deep in human lungs. Even in the rain. These tiny particles travel further and faster than we ever imagined, carried on winds, washed along rivers, and scattered like confetti across the globe.

In this chapter, we'll explore the weirdest spots microplastics have turned up, and just how far they've invaded our world.

"If microplastics were an Olympic sport,
they'd win gold in hide-and-seek —
they turn up everywhere you don't want them."

MICROPLASTICS IN RAINCLOUDS, ARCTIC SNOW, AND HUMAN LUNGS

Microplastics aren't content to just loiter in landfills or float about in rivers.

They're travellers, hitching rides on winds, waves, and water cycles to reach some of the most unexpected places on Earth — and even inside us.

RAINCLOUDS THAT SPRINKLE PLASTIC

When you picture rain, you probably think of fresh, clean water falling from the sky. But recent studies have revealed that rain isn't just water anymore — it's carrying **microplastics**.

How does that happen? Tiny fragments of plastic get blown into the air from car tyres, packaging, and industrial waste. They float upward on rising currents, mix with water droplets in clouds, and come back down as rainfall.

In one study, scientists estimated that millions of plastic particles rain down on cities every year — a sprinkle nobody asked for.

> *"Next time you're caught in a shower without an umbrella, remember: it's not just rain. It's a free top-up of microplastic seasoning. Adds crunch to your chips, if nothing else."*

SNOW IN THE ARCTIC

You'd think the Arctic, with its icy wilderness and miles of untouched snow, would be safe from plastic pollution. Sadly, no. Researchers drilling into fresh Arctic snow were stunned to find **high concentrations of microplastics**, carried there by winds from thousands of miles away.

Some of these tiny fragments likely came from Europe, Asia, or North America — proof that plastics don't respect borders. Once airborne, they can travel incredible distances, riding jet streams and weather systems until they settle in places that have never seen a crisp packet or a plastic straw.

Even the pristine white snow of the Arctic now has a hidden rainbow of plastic specks embedded in it.

PLASTIC IN HUMAN LUNGS

Perhaps the strangest and most unsettling discovery of all: **microplastics have been found inside human lungs.**

Scientists examined lung tissue and discovered tiny plastic fibres, probably inhaled from the air. Think about it — every time you breathe, you might be taking in invisible fragments shed from carpets, clothes, packaging, or car tyres.

And it doesn't stop there. Microplastics have also been found in human blood, placentas, and even breast milk. We don't yet know the full impact on our health, but the idea that we're walking around with plastic particles lodged inside us is more than a little unsettling.

> *"They say we're made of stardust, but at this rate, we're more like bin-dust. If I start coughing up Lego bricks, I'll know it's gone too far."*

*

From clouds above our heads to snow in the remotest corners of the planet, and right down into our lungs, microplastics have proven they're not just everywhere — they're *inside* everything.

Donny Wonder's Top 5 Strangest Microplastic Discoveries

Scientists are uncovering microplastics in places that make you scratch your head and mutter, *"How on earth did it get there?"* Here are my top five picks for the strangest (and slightly alarming) places these tiny particles have turned up.

1. In Human Blood

Yep, you read that right. Researchers recently detected microplastics floating in human bloodstreams.

That means plastic has gone from something we use to wrap sandwiches to something literally running through our veins.

> *"I always knew I had rock and roll in my blood.*
> *Turns out it's more like polythene."*

2. Inside Fresh Rain

From London to the Rocky Mountains, scientists have collected rainwater samples only to find them speckled with microplastics. It seems every time it rains, we're not just getting soaked — we're getting sprinkled with plastic confetti.

> *"Romantic kiss in the rain? Sure, but don't be*
> *surprised if your partner ends up with*
> *a microplastic moustache."*

3. In the Arctic and Antarctic Snow

Remote polar regions, thousands of miles from the nearest city, are no escape. Microplastics have been discovered in both Arctic and Antarctic snow, proving these little travellers go further than most humans will in a lifetime.

> *"Penguins and polar bears didn't sign up for this — their snow globes came with bonus sprinkles."*

4. In Beer and Salt

Two of humanity's favourite things — beer and salt — have both been found to contain microplastics. Sea salt carries fragments washed in from oceans, while beer picks them up through water supplies. Cheers?

Donny Wonder says:

"Great. Now my pint's got extra crunch. Who asked for a plastic chaser?"

5. On Mount Everest

Even the world's highest peak isn't safe. Climbers have left behind gear and litter, which break down into microplastics. Samples collected near Everest's summit revealed plastic fibres mingling with snow at the roof of the world.

> *"Forget planting a flag — humanity left its mark on Everest in the form of microscopic sock fluff."*

CLOSING THOUGHT

From our blood to our beer, from polar snow to mountain tops, microplastics have proven they can get *everywhere.* It's not just pollution anymore — it's infiltration.

> *"Microplastics don't need passports.*
> *They've gone global, and there's no customs official*
> *brave enough to stop them."*

CHAPTER 5
ANIMALS VS. PLASTIC

If humans are finding microplastics in their blood and beer, imagine what it's like for animals who don't get to choose what they eat or breathe. From the depths of the ocean to the skies above, wildlife is battling a problem they never asked for.

Sea turtles mistake plastic bags for jellyfish. Birds scoop up bottle caps and feed them to their chicks. Even tiny insects and earthworms are unknowingly carrying plastic into the soil beneath our feet.

For many creatures, plastic isn't just pollution — it's become part of their daily diet.

In this chapter, we'll look at how animals are coping (or not coping) with the rise of plastic in their world. It's sometimes tragic, sometimes strange, and occasionally so absurd you'll wonder if nature is playing a grim practical joke.

> *"The animal kingdom didn't invent plastic,*
> *but they're the ones choking on the bill."*

SEA TURTLES MISTAKING BAGS FOR JELLYFISH

Sea turtles have been gliding through oceans for more than 100 million years. They've survived the extinction of the dinosaurs, shifting climates, and countless natural predators. But in the last few decades, they've encountered a new, slippery threat: plastic bags.

To a turtle, a floating plastic bag looks almost identical to its favourite food — a jellyfish. Both are translucent, wobbly, and drift lazily through the water. Unfortunately, while jellyfish provide nutrition, plastic bags provide nothing but trouble.

When a turtle swallows a bag, the plastic can block its stomach or intestines, leaving the animal unable to digest real food. Even if it doesn't cause an immediate blockage, the bag can make the turtle feel full. That means the poor creature swims around thinking it's had dinner while slowly starving to death.

Research has shown just how widespread the problem is. Studies examining dead turtles often find their stomachs packed with plastic, sometimes dozens of items in a single animal. And it isn't just big bags — even small scraps of plastic film can cause deadly internal tangles.

The tragic irony? Humans invented single-use plastic bags only about 60 years ago. In less than a single turtle's lifetime, they've gone from a handy shopping convenience to a global ocean hazard.

> *"Imagine craving a juicy steak and biting into a rubber flip-flop instead. That's the turtle's dinner dilemma. Only difference is, you'd spit it out — they can't."*

There are some glimmers of hope. Bans on single-use plastic bags in many countries are helping reduce the number that reach the sea. Beach clean-ups and awareness campaigns are also making a difference. But for turtles, the fight isn't over — every discarded bag still looks like a tasty jellyfish, and they're not picky eaters.

The lesson here is simple: the bags we treat as "throwaway" can become death traps for creatures that have been thriving since prehistoric times.

BIRDS WITH PLASTIC BELLIES

If you've ever watched a seabird swoop over the ocean, you'll know how skilled they are at spotting food from above. But there's a catch: they're not always great at telling the difference between dinner and debris. To a hungry bird, a floating bottle cap, a shard of plastic, or a bright-coloured fragment can look just like a juicy morsel.

The result? Stomachs full of plastic.

Researchers studying seabirds have found staggering amounts of plastic in their bellies. One famous example comes from the **Laysan albatross** of Midway Atoll, in the Pacific Ocean.

Thousands of chicks die each year with stomachs stuffed with lighters, bottle caps, and bits of plastic packaging. Their parents, thinking they're feeding them fish and squid, unknowingly deliver a diet of rubbish.

Why do birds keep making this mistake? For one, plastic floats, just like fish eggs, squid, or other tasty treats. Many plastics also take on a fishy smell after drifting in seawater, making them even more appetising to a bird's sensitive nose. Bright colours don't help either — to a gull, a red straw or yellow fragment looks like easy prey.

The tragic part is that birds don't have a way to get rid of this plastic. Once swallowed, it just sits in their stomachs, taking up space that should be filled with food. Chicks, in particular, are vulnerable. With bellies full of bottle caps and toy fragments, they slowly starve, even as their parents keep feeding them more.

> *"Imagine sitting down to a delicious roast dinner only to find your plate covered in Lego and bottle caps. You wouldn't tuck in — but birds don't have the luxury of saying, 'Waiter, there's a toothbrush in my soup.'"*

Some species are hit harder than others. Studies estimate that by now, **over 90% of seabirds** have plastic inside them. And it's not just ocean birds — even garden species like sparrows and starlings have been found pecking at tiny plastic fragments in cities.

It's a global problem, but one that's waking people up. Campaigns against single-use plastics and littering are increasingly framed around these images of birds filled with rubbish. Because if an albatross chick can starve on a bellyful of bottle caps, it's hard for us to keep pretending plastic is harmless.

INSECTS AND WORMS CARRYING MICROPLASTICS INTO SOIL

When we think of microplastics, our minds usually go to oceans, beaches, and seabirds. But the problem isn't confined to water or the sky — it's creeping beneath our feet too. Soil, the very ground we grow our food in, is becoming a hiding place for plastic particles. And the culprits spreading them around? Some of the smallest creatures on Earth.

EARTHWORMS: NATURE'S RECYCLERS, NOW PLASTIC COURIERS

Earthworms are the gardeners of the natural world. They wriggle through soil, munching on organic matter and mixing nutrients as they go. But studies have shown that when microplastics are present in soil, worms accidentally eat them too.

What happens next is strange: the worms can actually **move the plastic deeper into the ground** as they burrow.

That means particles that might have sat harmlessly on the surface are dragged down into fertile layers where crops and plants grow. In one experiment, worms transported microplastics several centimetres into the soil in just a few weeks.

So instead of staying on the surface, plastic infiltrates the hidden underground world — all thanks to the very creatures meant to keep soil healthy.

INSECTS:
THE ACCIDENTAL TRANSPORTERS

Insects aren't immune either. Tiny soil-dwellers like springtails and beetles can carry microplastic fibres on their bodies or accidentally eat them along with organic matter.

Even pollinators like bees have been found carrying microplastic particles, picked up from flowers contaminated by air or water.

Every insect that nibbles, crawls, or digs becomes a potential courier, spreading plastic crumbs further into ecosystems. It's like nature's postal service, but instead of seeds and nutrients, the mailbag contains fragments of crisp packets.

WHY THIS MATTERS

Soil is the foundation of our food chain. If microplastics are being mixed into the earth by worms and insects, they can end up taken up by crops or leaching into groundwater. It's not just a problem for wildlife — it's a backdoor into our own food supply.

And unlike plastic in the ocean, which is visible in the tragic images of turtles and seabirds, plastic in the soil is out of sight and out of mind. Yet it may be just as damaging in the long run.

> *"Worms used to be the unsung heroes of the garden — turning muck into magic. Now they're moonlighting as delivery drivers for microplastics. Next time you see a worm wriggling in the rain, give it a nod. It's working hard, but carrying the wrong cargo."*

*

By the time you add up worms, insects, and other tiny critters, it's clear the microplastic problem isn't just floating in the oceans or drifting in the air. It's being shuffled underground, woven into the very fabric of the soil that sustains life. Which makes the next part of our journey all the more important: looking at how plastic affects animals both great and small.

CHAPTER 6
US VS. PLASTIC

It's one thing to see plastic tangled around a turtle or piling up in a bird's stomach. It's sad, shocking, and wrong — but at least it feels like their problem, out there in the wild. Except it isn't. Because microplastics aren't just in oceans, soils, or rainclouds anymore. They've made their way into *us*.

Scientists have discovered plastic particles in human blood, lung tissue, breast milk, and even in beer. We're breathing them, eating them, and drinking them without realising it. The material that once revolutionised our world is now quietly moving through our own bodies.

This chapter isn't about scaring you senseless — it's about shining a light on what's happening, what it could mean for our health, and how we can respond. We'll break down the facts, separate the hype from the science, and show you how plastic has become a very personal problem.

> *"You don't need to swim in the sea or lick a crisp packet to get microplastics in your system. Just being alive is enough. Congratulations, you're part human, part Tupperware."*

MICROPLASTICS IN BLOOD, BREAST MILK, AND BEER

Not long ago, the idea of plastic inside our bodies would've sounded like the plot of a dodgy sci-fi film. But today it's reality. Scientists have discovered microplastics in some of the most intimate and unexpected parts of human life — and it's forcing us to ask tough questions about just how deep this problem runs.

HUMAN BLOOD

In 2022, researchers tested blood samples from ordinary people and found microplastics in nearly **80% of them.** Tiny fragments of polyethylene (the stuff used in plastic bags) and PET (from drinks bottles) were drifting through the bloodstream like unwanted passengers.

This discovery raised eyebrows everywhere. If microplastics are floating through our blood, could they travel to our organs? Our brains? The truth is, scientists don't fully know yet. But the fact they're there at all is enough to make you glance suspiciously at your water bottle.

> *"They always said I was full of rubbish.*
> *Turns out, they were right."*

BREAST MILK

Even more sobering, studies have detected microplastics in human breast milk. That means newborn babies — the tiniest and most vulnerable among us — may be exposed to plastics from their very first feed.

Researchers aren't certain what this does to infants, but the discovery itself is unsettling. It shows just how unavoidable plastic exposure has become. From womb to cradle, it's part of our environment now.

BEER (AND SALT, AND MORE)

For those thinking, "Ah well, at least my pint is safe" — sorry. Microplastics have been found in beer, wine, and sea salt. They sneak in through contaminated water supplies and the ocean itself, making their way from plastic waste into the food and drink we enjoy.

One study tested 24 different beer brands and found microplastics in nearly all of them. Imagine raising a glass to celebrate the weekend only to discover you've just toasted with a sprinkle of plastic.

> *"I ordered a lager, not a lager-and-plastic combo.*
> *If I wanted extra crunch in my pint,*
> *I'd dunk a packet of crisps in it."*

*

From blood to breast milk to beer, microplastics have made it clear: there's no barrier they won't cross. We may not yet know the full consequences for human health, but one thing is certain — the plastic problem is no longer "out there." It's *in here.*

POSSIBLE HEALTH RISKS OF MICROPLASTICS

When scientists first started finding microplastics in humans, the immediate question was obvious: *what does this mean for our health?* Are we quietly turning into walking recycling bins? Or is it just another environmental nuisance that doesn't do much harm?

The honest answer is: we don't fully know yet. But researchers are racing to find out, and the clues so far suggest microplastics may not be as harmless as we'd like to think.

1. INFLAMMATION AND IRRITATION

Our bodies aren't designed to deal with plastic particles. When they end up in tissues — like the lungs or intestines — they can cause tiny injuries or inflammation. Think of it like having a splinter: small, irritating, and not life-threatening on its own. But if you had thousands of splinters scattered through your body, it wouldn't exactly be ideal.

Some studies suggest that when microplastics lodge in cells, the body treats them like intruders, sparking an immune response. Over time, constant irritation could add to stress on organs.

2. HITCHHIKING CHEMICALS

Plastics aren't just plastic. They're often made with additives like phthalates (used to make them flexible) or flame retardants (used to make them safer). Some of these chemicals are known to interfere with hormones or cause other health issues.

Microplastics can also act like little sponges, soaking up toxins and heavy metals from their surroundings. When swallowed or inhaled, those hitchhiking chemicals might come along for the ride. It's like eating a sponge that's soaked in washing-up liquid — the sponge itself is bad enough, but the chemicals it carries make it worse.

3. BREATHING THEM IN

We don't just eat microplastics — we breathe them, too. Dust in homes often contains plastic fibres from carpets, curtains, and clothes. One study found that a person might inhale tens of thousands of plastic particles each year.

For most people, the body's natural filters (like mucus and cilia in the lungs) catch many of these invaders. But some slip through and lodge deep in lung tissue. Over time, this might contribute to breathing problems, especially for people already vulnerable to conditions like asthma.

"I always knew London air was filthy, but I didn't expect it to come with a side order of polyester."

4. EFFECTS ON DIGESTION

Microplastics swallowed in food or drink can pass through the digestive system — but not always harmlessly. Some particles get stuck in the gut lining, where they can cause irritation. Others might interfere with how nutrients are absorbed, though research here is still in its early days.

Animal studies suggest that heavy microplastic exposure can stunt growth and affect reproduction. While humans aren't lab rats, the results do raise questions about what long-term exposure could do to us.

5. THE UNKNOWNS

Perhaps the biggest health risk of all is the **uncertainty.** Plastic is a relatively new invention in human history. Nobody has lived a full lifetime in a world where microplastics are this widespread. That means we don't yet know what decades of exposure will do.

Are they a nuisance our bodies can mostly shrug off? Or will future doctors look back at our generation and shake their heads, saying, "They should've seen it coming"?

At this point, science has more questions than answers — but enough concern to keep digging.

A BALANCED VIEW

It's important not to fall into panic. Microplastics aren't the new Black Death. But neither are they harmless. They're a daily drip-feed of a substance our bodies never evolved to handle, and that means caution is wise.

The good news? By learning where microplastics come from and how to reduce them, we can lower our exposure while also cutting the problem at its source. That's where the tips later in this book will come in handy.

> *"So far, science hasn't found proof that microplastics will turn us into superheroes — no sign of Plastic Man powers just yet. More likely, they're just giving our bodies a hard time, one invisible splinter at a time."*

SPOT THE SNEAKY PLASTIC

Alright, adventurers — time for a challenge. You've read about microplastics in oceans, animals, and even our own blood. Now it's your turn to play detective.

The Dare:

Try to go one whole day spotting where plastic sneaks into your life. Keep a notebook, use your phone, or just make mental notes. The goal isn't to feel guilty — it's to *see*.

Start when you wake up:

- Your toothbrush? Plastic.
- The toothpaste tube? Plastic.
- The shower gel bottle? Plastic.
- Even your clothes might be shedding microscopic fibres before you've had breakfast.

At work or school, check your lunch: crisp packets, drink bottles, coffee cups with sneaky plastic linings. At home, notice packaging, wrappers, bin bags, and the endless parade of containers. By bedtime, you'll probably be shocked at just how many times plastic popped up in your day.

Why do this? Because awareness is the first step. You can't dodge what you can't see. By spotting plastic, you start to understand where swaps, changes, or simple cutbacks can actually make a difference.

> *"Think of it like a treasure hunt —*
> *only the treasure is everywhere, and it's rubbish.*
> *Literally. But once you see it, you'll never unsee it."*

Are you ready to take the dare? Tomorrow, try being a plastic detective for a day. You'll find it's not about perfection — it's about noticing. And once you notice, you're already on the path to change.

PART 3
WHAT THE WORLD IS DOING

By now, we've seen just how far plastic has spread — from turtles choking on bags to microplastics floating in our bloodstreams. It's enough to make you want to crawl under a non-plastic rock and hide. But here's the good news: people all over the world are fighting back.

Governments, scientists, inventors, and everyday families are starting to say, *"Enough is enough."* From banning microbeads in face scrubs to charging for single-use bags, from giant river-cleaning machines to futuristic ideas like plastic-eating bacteria, the battle against plastic pollution has well and truly begun.

This part of the book looks at what's already being done, what's on the horizon, and whether it's actually making a difference.

Spoiler alert: it's a mixed bag (pun very much intended). Progress is real, but the problem is massive.

We'll explore victories like The Ocean Cleanup project, bans in the EU, UK, and US, and some truly weird but wonderful innovations — including mushrooms that can munch plastic like a midnight snack. Then we'll step back and ask the big question: **is it enough?**

> *"Humans made the mess,*
> *so humans should clean it up.*
> *Trouble is, we're still arguing about*
> *who's bringing the bin bags."*

So grab your metaphorical mop — it's time to see how the world is tackling the plastic peril, one law, one project, and one quirky invention at a time.

CHAPTER 7
THE FIGHT AGAINST PLASTIC

For decades, plastic looked unstoppable — cheap, durable, and everywhere. But eventually, the world began to wake up to the damage it was causing. Beaches buried in bottles, whales washing ashore with bellies full of bags, and scientists sounding alarms about microplastics in our food and water.

Bit by bit, governments, charities, and inventors started pushing back. Laws banning microbeads, charges for single-use bags, and huge cleanup projects like giant river "vacuum cleaners" began to shift the tide. And now, scientists are even experimenting with bizarre but brilliant ideas — from bacteria that can eat plastic to mushrooms that can break it down.

This chapter looks at how the fight began, how it's going, and the wild innovations that might just change the future.

"We built a plastic world. Now it's time to un-build it — preferably before the mushrooms beat us to it."

MICROBEAD BANS AND BAG CHARGES

Okay, so there's two things that need to be addressed here…

THE MICROBEAD MENACE

Back in the 1990s and early 2000s, cosmetic companies were obsessed with **microbeads** — tiny plastic spheres added to face scrubs, body washes, and even toothpaste. They were supposed to exfoliate your skin or give your teeth a dazzling polish. But there was a catch: once you rinsed them down the drain, they were too small for water treatment plants to filter out. Straight into rivers and oceans they went, adding billions of microscopic plastics to the environment every single day.

Fish, mussels, and other marine creatures swallowed them, mistaking them for food. And eventually, those same creatures ended up on our dinner plates. Not exactly the refreshing "deep clean" the adverts promised.

The public outcry was loud enough that governments took notice. In 2015, the United States passed the **Microbead-Free Waters Act**, banning their use in rinse-off cosmetics. The UK and several EU countries soon followed, phasing them out completely. Today, microbeads are largely a relic of bad product design — though their legacy is still washing around out there.

"Imagine brushing your teeth with glitter
and then being surprised it ended up everywhere.
Microbeads were like that — but sneakier."

THE BAG PROBLEM

If microbeads were the sneaky villain, **plastic bags** were the obvious one. Billions of them were being handed out every year in shops and supermarkets. Lightweight and flimsy, they often blew straight out of bins, drifted into rivers, and ended up strangling wildlife.

To combat this, governments began introducing charges for single-use bags. The idea was simple: make people pay a small fee — just a few pennies — and they'd start bringing their own reusable bags instead.

And it worked. In the UK, a 5p charge on plastic carrier bags (introduced in 2015 and later increased to 10p) slashed usage by more than **90% in major supermarkets.** Other countries, from Ireland to Kenya, have gone even further — some banning them outright.

The result? Far fewer flimsy bags drifting into hedges, waterways, and oceans. It proved that small changes in policy can make a big difference in behaviour.

> *"Turns out the best way to make people care about plastic bags wasn't to show them turtles choking on them — it was to charge 5p at the checkout. Nothing changes behaviour faster than hitting people in the wallet."*

*

Microbead bans and bag charges may not sound earth-shattering, but they showed the world that action is possible — and that even small steps can have huge impacts. They were the first cracks in plastic's armour.

GLOBAL PROJECTS AND GOVERNMENT BANS

Another couple of things...

THE OCEAN CLEANUP

When Dutch inventor **Boyan Slat** was just 18, he had an idea that sounded almost too ambitious: build massive floating systems to collect plastic from the ocean. Most people laughed it off. After all, the **Great Pacific Garbage Patch** is twice the size of Texas — who could possibly scoop that up?

But Slat didn't back down. He founded **The Ocean Cleanup**, a non-profit that now runs huge floating barriers designed to corral plastic into one place so it can be hauled out and recycled. The project also tackles rivers, using clever "Interceptor" machines to gobble up plastic before it ever reaches the sea.

It's not perfect — the ocean is huge, and plastic never stops flowing in — but it shows what happens when bold ideas meet determination. Instead of despairing at the size of the problem, The Ocean Cleanup is out there literally fishing for answers.

> *"Imagine a giant Hoover for the sea, but instead of sucking up biscuit crumbs from your carpet, it's slurping crisp packets out of the Pacific. Someone give that man a medal — or at least a reusable coffee cup."*

BANS AND LAWS: EU, UK, US, AND BEYOND

Governments across the globe are slowly catching on that plastic pollution isn't just an eyesore — it's an ecological disaster. That's led to a wave of bans, restrictions, and regulations aimed at cutting down on the worst offenders.

- **The European Union** banned a range of single-use plastics in 2021, including straws, cutlery, plates, and polystyrene food containers. The idea? Eliminate items that are cheap to make, easy to lose, and disastrous for wildlife.

- **The UK** followed suit, introducing similar bans on straws, stirrers, and cotton buds, alongside earlier charges for plastic bags. In 2023, England also banned single-use plastic cutlery and plates, pushing people toward reusable alternatives.

- **The United States** has a patchwork approach, with some states and cities leading the charge. California, for instance, banned plastic bags statewide, while other regions are phasing out foam containers and single-use straws.

- **Other countries** have gone even bolder. Kenya introduced one of the strictest plastic bag bans in the world, with hefty fines (or even jail time) for anyone caught producing or using them.

These laws aren't perfect — plenty of plastic still slips through — but they show that with enough pressure, governments can act. And once they do, consumer habits start to shift.

> *"Governments banning plastic straws was a nice start. But honestly, turtles don't care if your mojito comes with a bamboo straw if the rest of the ocean still looks like a skip."*

*

Together, bold projects like The Ocean Cleanup and sweeping bans across continents mark the first real signs of a global response. They don't solve everything — not even close — but they prove that change is possible when people decide plastic isn't worth the price we're paying.

THE WILD FUTURE: PLASTIC-EATING BACTERIA AND MUSHROOMS

If humans made the plastic mess, maybe nature can help clean it up. In recent years, scientists have discovered some truly bizarre allies in the fight against plastic — living organisms that don't just tolerate plastic, they *eat* it.

BACTERIA WITH A TASTE FOR BOTTLES

In 2016, Japanese researchers studying a recycling plant stumbled upon a species of bacteria that had evolved a brand-new trick: it could break down PET, the plastic used in drinks bottles. They named it **Ideonella sakaiensis**.

This microbe produces special enzymes that chop PET into smaller chemical pieces, which the bacteria can then digest for energy. In other words, it snacks on plastic. Since then, scientists have tweaked and "supercharged" the enzymes in the lab, making them thousands of times faster at breaking down bottles.

Some experiments suggest they could reduce a bottle to its building blocks in just a few days.

It's not quite ready for large-scale use — but the idea of an enzyme-based recycling system is no longer science fiction. Instead of plastic lasting centuries, bacteria could one day turn it back into raw materials in a matter of weeks.

> *"Trust humans to invent something that lasts forever, only for bacteria to turn up and say, 'Hold my petri dish.'"*

MUSHROOMS THAT MUNCH PLASTIC

As if hungry bacteria weren't strange enough, fungi have also joined the fight.

In 2011, scientists in Ecuador discovered a species of mushroom called **Pestalotiopsis microspora** that can break down polyurethane (a type of plastic used in foams, coatings, and adhesives). Even more astonishing: it can do this **without oxygen.** That means it could survive munching away at plastic buried deep in landfills.

Since then, other fungi have been tested and shown promise in nibbling on different types of plastics. Mycelium (the root-like networks fungi use) has also been explored as a sustainable replacement for packaging — a kind of "grown" alternative to Styrofoam.

Imagine a future where mushrooms not only grow in forests but also quietly clean up rubbish dumps. They might not sprout out of old crisp packets just yet, but the potential is there.

OTHER WILD IDEAS

- **Waxworms:** These little caterpillars have enzymes in their guts that can break down polyethylene (the stuff used in plastic bags). Unfortunately, they also really like chewing holes in beehives, so they're not exactly eco-heroes yet.

- **Engineered Enzymes:** Beyond natural discoveries, scientists are designing synthetic enzymes that could gobble plastic even faster. Think of it as nature's toolkit, turbocharged by human tinkering.

- **Plastic-Eating "Super Soils":** Some researchers are even experimenting with engineered compost heaps where microbes and fungi work together to dismantle plastic waste like a team of microscopic demolition experts.

A NOTE OF CAUTION

These discoveries are exciting, but they're not magic bullets. Plastic-eating bacteria and mushrooms work best in controlled lab conditions. Scaling them up to tackle mountains of waste is still a massive challenge. Plus, we need to make sure the cure doesn't cause new problems — nobody wants a runaway fungus happily chewing on their garden furniture.

But the message is clear: nature is adapting. And with a little help from science, the living world might just hold the keys to undoing some of the damage we've caused.

"First, bacteria learn to eat our bottles. Next, mushrooms munch through landfills. If bread starts growing mould that eats crisp packets, I'm moving to Mars."

CHAPTER 8
IS IT ENOUGH?

We've seen governments ban microbeads, shoppers swap plastic bags for reusable totes, inventors build giant ocean hoovers, and even mushrooms nibble on foam. It sounds impressive — and it *is.*

But here's the big question: with plastic production still climbing every year, is all of this actually enough to turn the tide?

The truth is complicated. For every success story, there's a sobering reminder of the sheer scale of the problem. Billions of tonnes of plastic already exist, and millions more are being made daily. Progress is real, but plastic isn't giving up its crown without a fight.

In this chapter, we'll take an honest but hopeful look at where the world stands. We'll weigh the victories against the challenges, and for fun, we'll even keep score: **Humans vs. Plastic — who's winning?**

> *"We've landed punches, sure.*
> *But plastic's still in the ring, smirking,*
> *with its gloves made out of itself."*

IS IT ENOUGH?
THE HONEST BUT HOPEFUL TRUTH

Plastic pollution is one of those problems where the numbers are both mind-boggling and, frankly, depressing. Scientists estimate that humans have produced over **8 billion tonnes of plastic** since the 1950s. Of that, less than 10% has ever been recycled.

The rest has been burned, buried, or is still out there — in oceans, rivers, soils, and the air we breathe. And here's the kicker: global plastic production is still *increasing*. By 2050, some projections say there could be more plastic in the ocean (by weight) than fish.

That sounds like a knockout blow in Plastic's favour. But here's where the hope sneaks in: we *are* fighting back.

WHERE WE'RE WINNING

- **Behavioural Shifts:** Bag charges have shown that small policies can lead to massive cultural change. Millions of flimsy bags are no longer littering our streets and beaches.
- **Public Awareness:** Plastic has gone from a boring packaging issue to a front-page story. Everyone from school kids to world leaders knows about turtles and straws. Awareness drives action.
- **Innovations:** From The Ocean Cleanup to plastic-eating enzymes, ideas that once sounded wacky are now being tested in labs and rivers around the world.

- **Policy Momentum:** The EU, UK, US (in parts), and dozens of other countries are putting bans and restrictions in place. It's patchy, but the tide is turning.

WHERE WE'RE STRUGGLING

- **Sheer Volume:** For every bag we ban, industries churn out billions of new bottles, wrappers, and packaging. Demand is still sky-high.
- **Recycling Gaps:** Most plastics are still not recyclable in practice, even if they have that little triangle logo on them. Many end up incinerated or in landfills.
- **Global Inequality:** Wealthier countries can afford cleanup projects and bans. Poorer nations often bear the brunt of plastic pollution without the same resources to tackle it.
- **Invisible Threats:** Microplastics are far harder to control than bottles on beaches. They're already everywhere — and no ban or cleanup project can undo what's already scattered across the planet.

THE BALANCING ACT

So, is it enough? Not yet. The scale of the problem is still bigger than the solutions we've built. But that doesn't mean we're powerless. Every ban, every invention, every clean-up effort slows the tide and buys time for bigger shifts.

What's hopeful is that once people *do* act, the results can be dramatic. Bag charges dropped usage by more than 90%. Microbead bans eliminated billions of particles a day. Ocean-cleaning tech is pulling tonnes of rubbish from rivers. These are proof-of-concept victories — signs that humans *can* change behaviour and bend systems when we want to.

The key is momentum. The more people push, the more governments regulate, and the more scientists innovate, the closer we get to turning the tide.

> *"Right now, it's like trying to bail out a sinking ship*
> *with a teacup. But hey — we've started.*
> *Swap that teacup for a bucket, and then for a pump,*
> *and suddenly the ship's got a fighting chance."*

HUMANS VS. PLASTIC: WHO'S WINNING?

Sometimes the best way to make sense of a big, messy fight is to keep score. So let's imagine this as a boxing match: **Humans vs. Plastic.** Round after round, punch after punch — who's ahead?

Round 1: Awareness

- **Humans:** Plastic is no longer invisible. Campaigns, documentaries, and viral turtle videos have made it a household issue. Kids in classrooms know about microplastics before they know long division. Big win.

- **Plastic:** Still sneaks into our lives daily, hidden in packaging, clothes, and tyres. Out of sight, out of mind — until it's not.

Score: Humans 1 – Plastic 1

Round 2: Laws and Bans

- **Humans:** Microbead bans, bag charges, straw restrictions, and single-use cutlery bans. Proof that governments can act. Usage drops fast when they do.
- **Plastic:** The plastics industry still produces millions of tonnes annually, and lobbyists fight tooth and nail against stronger regulations.

Score: Humans 2 – Plastic 2

Round 3: Cleanups and Innovations

- **Humans:** The Ocean Cleanup hauls tonnes of rubbish out of rivers. Enzyme research could make recycling faster. Fungi and bacteria are nibbling away at the problem.
- **Plastic:** For every tonne removed, thousands more are produced. Cleanups are heroic, but they're still a drop in the ocean — literally.

Score: Humans 3 – Plastic 4

Round 4: Health and Environment

- **Humans:** Growing awareness means scientists are racing to understand microplastic health risks, which may drive policy changes.
- **Plastic:** Already in our blood, breast milk, lungs, and food. Wildlife is choking on it. Microplastics are everywhere, and we can't remove what's already scattered.

Score: Humans 3 – Plastic 5

Final Score

Plastic is still in the lead. Its durability, cheapness, and sheer volume give it the advantage. But here's the twist: this isn't a fight we can just throw in the towel on. Because we're not spectators — we're in the ring.

And if history shows anything, it's that humans can be scrappy fighters when pushed. We've cracked polio, split the atom, and landed on the Moon. Beating plastic won't be easy, but it's far from impossible.

> *"Plastic's ahead on points, but Humans have got grit.*
> *If this goes to the final round, I'm betting on*
> *the underdog with opposable thumbs."*

PART 4
WHAT YOU CAN DO

We've travelled through the history of plastic, zoomed in on microplastics, and looked at what the world is doing to fight back. But here's the bit that really matters: what can *you* do?

Because while governments pass laws and scientists tinker with plastic-eating mushrooms, the truth is that change also starts in homes, classrooms, and supermarkets. Every swap, every habit, every mindful choice chips away at the problem. No, you can't solve plastic pollution single-handedly.

But you *can* make a dent — and when millions of people do the same, dents become cracks, and cracks become real change.

This part of the book is all about practical, everyday action. We'll look at simple **plastic-free swaps** you can make around the house, fun ways to turn your family into **plastic detectives**, and easy lifestyle tweaks that add up to a **plastic-light life** without feeling like punishment.

And because this is a Donny Wonder book, we're going to keep it playful. Expect checklists, dares, and even a game of "Plastic Swap Bingo." Saving the planet might be serious, but nobody said it can't be fun.

> *"Think of it like a camping trip...*
> *If everyone leaves just a little less mess behind,*
> *the whole campsite stays beautiful.*
> *Plus, nobody has to sit on*
> *a discarded crisp packet."*

So let's roll up our sleeves (reusable ones, obviously) and see what swaps, games, and dares you can take on in your own life.

CHAPTER 9
PLASTIC-FREE SWAPS

Going plastic-free can sound intimidating, like you need to live in a cave weaving clothes from nettles. But the truth is, most swaps are simple, affordable, and even fun once you start spotting them. A bamboo toothbrush here, a solid shampoo bar there, and suddenly your bathroom looks less like a plastic jungle and more like an eco-friendly spa.

In this chapter, we'll explore easy **household hacks** that cut down plastic without cutting out comfort. And to keep things playful, Donny Wonder has cooked up a game of **"Plastic Swap Bingo"** — a checklist of swaps that turns eco-living into a challenge you'll actually enjoy.

> *"It's not about being perfect. It's about swapping the stuff that makes sense — and giving yourself a little victory dance every time you win a round of Bingo."*

HOUSEHOLD HACKS FOR A PLASTIC-LIGHTER LIFE

Going plastic-free doesn't mean tossing out everything you own and starting from scratch. It's about making smart swaps — little changes that replace throwaway items with longer-lasting, kinder alternatives. Think of it as upgrading your toolkit for everyday life.

BAMBOO TOOTHBRUSHES

Every plastic toothbrush you've ever used still exists somewhere. Billions of them are clogging landfills and oceans. The easy fix? **Bamboo toothbrushes.** They work just as well, feel just as sturdy, and when you're done, the handle can go in the compost. (Just pull out the nylon bristles first.)

SOLID SHAMPOO BARS

Bottles of shampoo are one of the sneakiest sources of bathroom plastic. Enter the **shampoo bar**: a solid block that lasts as long as two or three bottles, comes in cardboard packaging (or sometimes none at all), and often smells like heaven.

Bonus: they're great for travel — no risk of leaks in your luggage.

REFILL SHOPS

More and more towns have **zero-waste or refill shops** where you can take your own containers and stock up on pasta, rice, flour, cereal, coffee, washing-up liquid, or even peanut butter. It cuts out the endless parade of plastic packaging and turns shopping into something a little more adventurous.

REUSABLE BOTTLES AND CUPS

This one's a classic, but it makes a huge dent. A stainless steel or glass bottle can last years, keeping drinks hot or cold without single-use plastic bottles piling up.

The same goes for reusable coffee cups — many cafés even give you a discount for bringing your own.

CLOTH BAGS AND PRODUCE BAGS

Swap single-use bags for sturdy cloth totes. Add a few lightweight mesh produce bags for fruit and veg, and suddenly you're not bringing home armfuls of crinkly plastic film every week.

BEESWAX WRAPS

Cling film is one of those kitchen plastics that feels unavoidable — until you meet **beeswax wraps.** Made from cotton coated in beeswax, they're flexible, reusable, and mould to whatever you cover (sandwiches, bowls, cheese). Wash them gently and they last for months.

BAR SOAP AND TOOTHPASTE TABLETS

Bottled hand soap and plastic toothpaste tubes are easy swaps.

Go old-school with bar soap (there are hundreds of lovely eco brands now), or try **toothpaste tablets** that come in refillable tins. Pop one in your mouth, chew, brush, and grin at your plastic-free pearly whites.

LAUNDRY HACKS

- **Soap nuts** (dried fruit shells that release natural detergent).

- **Laundry sheets or powder in cardboard boxes** instead of plastic bottles.

- **A Guppyfriend bag** (or similar) to catch synthetic fibres from clothes in the wash before they escape into waterways.

KITCHEN UPGRADES

- Switch to **stainless steel lunch boxes** or **glass containers** instead of flimsy tubs.

- Use **wooden or metal utensils** instead of plastic spatulas that melt on hot pans.

- Try a **French press or stovetop coffee maker** instead of pod machines that churn out plastic waste.

TOILET PAPER & TISSUES

Plastic-wrapped loo rolls are everywhere, but plenty of brands now sell paper wrapped in paper. Some even deliver in bulk with zero plastic packaging. Same goes for tissues — cardboard boxes beat plastic packs.

CLEANING PRODUCTS

Refillable sprays, concentrated cleaners (just add water), or DIY mixes (vinegar + bicarb = magic) all beat the endless buying of new plastic spray bottles.

THE HACK MENTALITY

The secret to plastic-light living is this: don't try to swap *everything* at once. Pick one or two hacks that make sense for your life, get comfortable with them, then add another. Before long, your home looks less like a plastic jungle and more like a clever, sustainable toolkit.

> *"Plastic-free swaps aren't about living like a monk. They're about finding smarter gear for the adventure of daily life. And if your toothbrush looks cooler in bamboo than in neon pink plastic, that's a bonus."*

DONNY WONDER'S PLASTIC SWAP BINGO

Want to make plastic swaps more fun? Play **Bingo** with your own life. Each time you make a swap, tick it off. Get all five in a category, and you've scored a win against plastic. Go for a full house, and you're basically an eco-legend.

Here's the Donny Wonder version:

Bathroom Bingo

- ☐ Swap plastic toothbrush → **bamboo toothbrush**
- ☐ Ditch shampoo bottles → **solid shampoo bar**
- ☐ Replace shower gel → **bar soap**
- ☐ Try **toothpaste tablets** instead of plastic tubes
- ☐ Use a **safety razor** instead of disposable ones

Kitchen Bingo

- ☐ Swap cling film → **beeswax wraps or silicone lids**
- ☐ Use **glass jars or metal tins** instead of plastic tubs
- ☐ Switch to **wooden/metal cooking utensils**
- ☐ Buy in bulk or refill → **pasta, rice, beans, oats**
- ☐ Use **reusable lunchboxes and cutlery** instead of disposables

On-the-Go Bingo

- ☐ Carry a **reusable water bottle**
- ☐ Bring your own **coffee cup** to cafés
- ☐ Keep a **cloth shopping bag** in your car or backpack
- ☐ Say "no" to plastic straws → use **metal, bamboo, or none at all**
- ☐ Choose snacks with **paper or no packaging** instead of plastic wrappers

---

Laundry & Cleaning Bingo

- ☐ Catch microfibres with a **Guppyfriend bag** or filter
- ☐ Swap detergent bottles → **powder, sheets, or soap nuts**
- ☐ Try **DIY vinegar + bicarb cleaner** instead of plastic sprays
- ☐ Reuse old T-shirts as **cleaning cloths** instead of buying plastic-packaged wipes
- ☐ Buy **plastic-free toilet rolls** (paper wrapped or bulk delivery)

Bonus Round: Eco-Hero Moves

- ☐ Visit a **refill shop** with your own jars and bottles
- ☐ Host a **swap party** with friends (clothes, toys, books — less packaging all round)

- ☐ Gift items in **reusable wrapping** (like cloth or boxes)
- ☐ Switch glitter → **biodegradable glitter**
- ☐ Plant herbs or veg in **upcycled containers** instead of plastic pots

---

How to Play

- One in a category = **Plastic Rookie**
- Two in a category = **Plastic Pro**
- Full house = **Donny Wonder Approved Eco-Champion**

> *"Saving the planet doesn't have to be a lecture. Turn it into a game, tick some boxes, and give yourself a fist pump when you win. Bonus points if you shout BINGO loud enough for the neighbours to wonder what's going on."*

CHAPTER 10
FAMILY PLASTIC DETECTIVE

Think Sherlock Holmes with a magnifying glass. Only instead of solving crimes, you're solving the mystery of where plastic sneaks into your home. The truth is, most of us don't realise just how many bits of plastic we use every day — from food packaging to bathroom bottles, from hidden linings in coffee cups to those clingy produce bags at the supermarket.

That's where the **Plastic Detective** game comes in. Together as a family, you'll do a "plastic audit": hunting through cupboards, shelves, and bins to spot the culprits. And because everything's better with a bit of competition, you'll turn it into a game with points, prizes, and maybe a little bragging rights.

The goal isn't to feel guilty — it's to *see.* Once you spot the sneaky plastics, you can start swapping them out for smarter choices.

And you'll have a laugh while you're at it!

> *"Detectives never solve mysteries by
> ignoring the clues. Grab your magnifying glass
> and get nosy — because plastic's hiding everywhere,
> and it thinks you won't catch it."*

HOW TO DO A HOUSEHOLD PLASTIC AUDIT

A **plastic audit** is basically a treasure hunt — except instead of gold coins, you're spotting bottles, wrappers, and sneaky plastics that have quietly invaded your home. The idea is simple: track where plastic shows up in your daily life, then figure out which ones you can swap, reduce, or ditch.

Here's how to turn it into a proper detective mission.

Step 1: Gather Your Detective Tools

Before you start, arm yourself with:

- **A notebook or chart** (or a whiteboard for maximum drama).
- **Coloured pens or stickers** for scoring.
- **Magnifying glasses** (optional, but they make kids feel like Sherlock Holmes).
- **Team spirit** — this is about spotting, not shaming.

Step 2: Choose Your Zones

Split the house into "crime scenes":

- Kitchen
- Bathroom
- Living room
- Bedrooms
- Laundry area
- Garden / garage (if you've got one)

Tackle one zone at a time so it doesn't feel overwhelming.

Step 3: The Hunt Begins

As a family, sweep through each zone and write down every item that contains plastic. Some are obvious — bottles, bags, wrappers. Others are sneaky — lids, labels, linings. Encourage kids to poke around and be curious.

Detective tip: Pick up things you wouldn't expect. Did you know that most teabags are heat-sealed with plastic? Or that receipts sometimes have a plastic coating?

Step 4: Sort Into Categories

Once you've gathered your suspects, sort them into three lists:

1. **Single-use plastics** — cling film, straws, disposable cutlery, wrappers.
2. **Long-term plastics** — toothbrushes, shampoo bottles, lunchboxes, detergent bottles.
3. **Hidden plastics** — teabags, coffee cup linings, glitter, clothes made of polyester or nylon.

This makes it easier to see which swaps are quick wins (single-use) and which will take more thought.

Step 5: Count and Score

Turn it into a competition. Award points for each plastic item spotted:

- 1 point = obvious plastic (bottle, bag).

- 2 points = sneaky plastic (teabag, toothpaste tube).
- 3 points = bonus discovery (something nobody else realised was plastic).

Whoever racks up the most points gets bragging rights as **Chief Plastic Detective.**

Step 6: Spot the Big Offenders

At the end of your audit, look at your lists. Which items appeared most often? Packaging? Bottles? Clothes fibres?

These are your **"repeat offenders."** Put a star next to them — they'll be the best place to start making swaps.

Step 7: Choose Easy Swaps

Now the fun part. For each repeat offender, brainstorm a swap. Example:

- Plastic toothbrush → bamboo toothbrush.
- Shampoo bottle → shampoo bar.
- Cling film → beeswax wraps.
- Plastic produce bag → mesh bag.
- Polyester jumper shedding fibres → laundry bag that catches them.

Keep it realistic — one or two swaps at a time is enough.

Step 8: Re-Audit Later

A detective never closes the case after the first clue. Do another audit in a month. See if your plastic use has gone down. Celebrate progress, no matter how small.

Why This Works

A plastic audit isn't about guilt. It's about awareness. Once you actually see the amount of plastic sneaking into your daily life, you can't unsee it.

That makes you far more likely to change habits — and kids especially love spotting the hidden culprits.

> *"Think of it like a board game, only instead of landing on snakes or ladders, you land on shampoo bottles and crisp packets. Whoever finds the most wins — but in this game, the planet wins too."*

TURN IT INTO A GAME: POINTS FOR SPOTTING SNEAKY PLASTIC

If you want your family to actually enjoy a plastic audit, don't frame it as a chore — frame it as a game.

The goal is to **make spotting plastic fun, surprising, and a little competitive.**

Here's how to gamify your audit:

1. Detective Ranks

Give every player a "detective title" to kick things off:

- Rookie Plastic Spotter
- Inspector Bottle-Cap
- Sergeant Straw
- Chief Detective Recyclo
- The ultimate title: **Plastic Buster General** (reserved for the top scorer).

Kids (and let's be honest, adults too) will love trying to climb the ranks.

2. Scoring System

Not all plastic is created equal, so make the points reflect how sneaky the item is:

- **1 point:** Obvious plastic (water bottle, bag, yoghurt pot).
- **2 points:** Everyday plastic people often overlook (toothpaste tubes, crisp packets, teabags, receipts).
- **3 points:** "Aha!" discoveries — hidden or unusual plastics nobody else noticed (polyester in clothes, glitter, coffee cup linings, chewing gum).

You can even add **bonus points** for the grossest find (plastic lurking in the bin) or the funniest (like a toy that's 99% plastic pretending to be a "nature animal").

3. Mini-Missions

Spice it up with detective challenges:

- **The Kitchen Caper:** Who can find the most plastic in the fridge and cupboards?
- **Bathroom Bust:** How many bottles or wrappers are hiding on the shelves?
- **Bin Bag Bonus:** Carefully (and safely) spot how much of today's rubbish is plastic.
- **The Wardrobe Whodunnit:** Which clothes are secretly synthetic fibres?

Each mission can be timed with a stopwatch for extra suspense.

4. Rewards and Forfeits

At the end, tally the points. The winner gets a fun eco-themed prize (like choosing the next plastic-free swap the family will try). The lowest scorer does a silly forfeit — maybe singing a "Plastic Blues" song or doing a dramatic reading of the back of a cereal packet.

5. Keep a Scoreboard

Make it a series instead of a one-off. Put a scoreboard on the fridge and track family detective points over a week or a month. Each new audit becomes another round in the ongoing **Plastic Detective Championship.**

6. Celebrate the Wins

When the family spots repeat offenders, cheer them on. Clap, shout "Bingo!", or even play a silly victory sound effect. The more fun you make it, the more memorable it becomes — and the more likely the swaps will stick.

WHY IT WORKS

Turning the audit into a game transforms it from a nagging eco-task into an adventure. Kids love hunting for sneaky plastics, parents get competitive, and everyone walks away more aware of what's sneaking into their lives.

> *"Plastic is sneaky, but humans are sneakier when there are points on the line. Nothing brings out true detective spirit like the promise of victory and a silly prize."*

CHAPTER 11
LIVING THE
PLASTIC-LIGHT LIFE

By now, you've swapped your toothbrush, scouted your bathroom bottles, and maybe even shouted "BINGO!" at your sandwich wraps. You're officially on the path to using less plastic. But the real trick isn't just one-off swaps or family games — it's building habits that stick.

Living a "plastic-light" life doesn't mean living in a yurt and weaving socks out of nettles. It's about finding **easy, everyday changes** that deliver big results without sucking the joy out of life. Think: using a washing bag to catch microfibres from clothes, avoiding glitter that lingers longer than your last birthday balloon, or buying in bulk to cut down on endless packaging. Small tweaks, big impact.

And because no Donny Wonder chapter is complete without a challenge, you'll finish with a **Plastic Dare**: surviving an entire weekend without single-use plastic. Spoiler: it's trickier than you think, but eye-opening in all the right ways.

> *"Plastic is like that clingy friend who turns up everywhere uninvited. The goal isn't to ghost them completely — it's to set some boundaries."*

EASY THINGS WITH BIG IMPACT

Sometimes the biggest wins come from the smallest changes. You don't need to overhaul your entire lifestyle to make a difference — you just need to know where the sneakiest plastics are and how to tackle them. Here are a few simple shifts that pack a powerful punch.

1. WASHING BAGS FOR CLOTHES

Here's a fact most people don't know: when you wash synthetic clothes (like polyester, nylon, or fleece), they shed **tiny plastic fibres**. These microfibres slip through washing machines and end up in rivers and oceans, adding to the microplastic problem.

Enter the **washing bag** (like the Guppyfriend). Pop your clothes inside before throwing them in the machine, and it traps the fibres before they escape. Some people also use filters that attach to their washing machine hoses to catch the fibres.

It's an easy hack that turns laundry day into a secret act of eco-heroism.

> *"I used to think my fleece jumper was cosy.*
> *Turns out it's also a plastic snowstorm*
> *waiting to happen. Who knew?"*

2. AVOIDING GLITTER

Glitter looks fun, but under the microscope it's just **tiny bits of plastic** that never disappear. Those shiny specks wash down sinks, float into rivers, and sparkle forever in places they shouldn't — like inside fish gills.

The good news? You don't need to give up the sparkle. Loads of companies now make **biodegradable glitter** from plant cellulose. It looks just as fabulous at festivals, parties, and craft time, but it actually breaks down instead of hanging around until the apocalypse.

Swap plastic glitter for the biodegradable kind and you'll save yourself from sprinkling microplastics every time you craft a birthday card.

3. BUYING IN BULK

Packaging is one of the biggest culprits in household plastic waste. Pasta, rice, lentils, oats, snacks, detergent — they all come in endless plastic bags and bottles. Buying in bulk solves two problems at once: it reduces plastic and saves money.

Options include:

- **Refill shops:** Bring your own jars and fill up with dried goods, oils, or even cleaning products.
- **Bulk packs:** Choose giant bags or boxes instead of lots of smaller ones — one sack of rice beats 20 little plastic packets.

- **Big bottles of detergent:** Better one big container than ten little ones. Bonus points if you refill.

Bulk buying cuts down packaging and reduces the carbon footprint of repeated deliveries and production. Plus, there's something satisfying about seeing a huge jar of oats lined up on the shelf.

> *"Buy pasta like you're feeding an army,*
> *and suddenly you're not swimming in plastic packets*
> *every week. Just don't forget to actually eat it —*
> *nobody wants a cupboard full of guilt spaghetti."*

OTHER EASY WINS TO ADD TO YOUR TOOLKIT

- **Choose loose fruit and veg** over plastic-wrapped ones (bonus: it often tastes fresher).
- **Use matches or refillable lighters** instead of disposable plastic lighters.
- **Switch to tea in loose-leaf or biodegradable bags** — many standard teabags are sealed with plastic.
- **Pick cardboard-packaged items** (like laundry powder or cereal) over plastic tubs.
- **Share or borrow instead of buy new** — tools, toys, books, even clothes. Less packaging, less waste.

THE BOTTOM LINE

Each of these swaps is small, but the impact adds up fast. Washing bags stop invisible microfibres. Glitter swaps prevent thousands of shiny specks from sneaking into rivers. Bulk buying slashes packaging waste. Do even one of them and you're already shifting the balance.

> *"Plastic is stubborn, but it's not invincible.*
> *Chip away at it with smart little hacks,*
> *and soon enough, you've turned a mountain into*
> *a molehill — and a glitter-free mole at that."*

SURVIVE A WEEKEND WITHOUT SINGLE-USE PLASTIC

Okay, eco-detectives — time for the ultimate test. You've learned the swaps, played Bingo, and sniffed out the sneaky plastics. Now it's challenge time:

Can you survive an entire weekend without single-use plastic?

The Rules

1. From Friday evening to Sunday night, **say no to single-use plastics.**
2. That means no plastic bottles, no takeaway tubs, no straws, no cling film, no shiny snack wrappers.
3. If you absolutely can't avoid something (say, your medicine comes in a blister pack), don't panic —

just *note it down*. The goal isn't perfection, it's awareness.

4. Keep a little logbook (or your phone notes app) to track every success, every slip, and every sneaky plastic ambush.

What to Expect

- **The easy wins:** Swapping bottled water for your reusable flask, using beeswax wraps instead of cling film, and carrying a cloth bag for shopping.
- **The tricky bits:** Snacks, takeaway food, and unexpected culprits like receipts, tea bags, or pre-wrapped cucumbers.
- **The lightbulb moments:** Realising how many times you almost grabbed plastic without thinking — and how satisfying it feels to dodge it.

Make It Fun

- Turn it into a family challenge: who can rack up the fewest plastic "slip-ups"?
- Add dares: loser has to do the recycling dance in the kitchen.
- Share your victories: post your plastic-free meals or clever hacks online and inspire others.

WHY THIS MATTERS

Two days might not sound like much, but it's long enough to reveal just how woven into daily life plastic has become. More importantly, it shows you which areas are hardest to tackle — the places where swaps or new habits will have the biggest impact.

> *"Think of it like camping in the wild.*
> *You don't bring twenty bottles of water*
> *and a mountain of cling film sandwiches.*
> *You strip it back, get clever, and make do.*
> *Survive a weekend without plastic and you'll see*
> *— it's not only possible, it's kind of fun."*

*

By the end of the dare, you won't just have survived a plastic-light weekend — you'll have spotted the sneaky plastics that creep into your life most often. And once you see them, you'll know exactly where to strike next.

PART 5
FUN WITH RECYCLING

By now, you've seen the dark side of plastic and learned how to dodge it in daily life. But here's the twist: not all plastic has to be the villain. With a little imagination, those bottles, caps, and tubs cluttering your cupboards can be transformed into something colourful, useful, or downright silly.

This part of the book is all about turning **trash into treasure** — making recycling fun, creative, and a little bit daft. Indoors, you'll try your hand at crafty projects like **bottle cap mosaics**, **milk jug masks**, and **plastic-bottle lanterns** that bring light (literally) to the plastic problem.

Donny Wonder will throw in a few ridiculous "Wonder Full" challenges along the way to keep you laughing while you glue your fingers together.

Outdoors, you'll take recycling into the garden with projects that blend sustainability and playfulness. From **bottle-built greenhouses** and **DIY plant pots** to **drip irrigation hacks** and even a **scarecrow in a Donny Wonder hat**, you'll find creative ways to put old plastic to work in growing new life.

Because recycling doesn't have to be boring or guilt-ridden. It can be fun, messy, colourful, and a brilliant excuse to get crafty with the kids (or competitive with the neighbours).

> *"If the world's drowning in plastic,*
> *we might as well build something wonderful*
> *out of it — even if it's just a lantern that looks*
> *like a dragon or a scarecrow with better hair than me."*

CHAPTER 12
ARTS & CRAFTS INDOORS

When most people think of recycling, they picture sorting bins and trudging to the bottle bank. But recycling can also mean rolling up your sleeves, grabbing some glue, and turning rubbish into something surprisingly brilliant. Indoors, plastic isn't just waste — it's raw material for creativity.

In this chapter, you'll explore crafty ways to give plastic a second life. You'll make colourful **bottle cap mosaics**, transform old milk jugs into **helmets and masks**, and cut and twist bottles into glowing **lanterns**. None of these projects need fancy tools or expensive supplies — just imagination, a willingness to get a bit messy, and a sense of humour when things don't go quite as planned.

And because this is a Donny Wonder book, you'll also face a few **"Wonder Full" craft challenges** — silly side quests with daft commentary designed to keep you laughing while you craft. Think less "Pinterest perfection" and more "eco-friendly chaos with character."

> *"Crafting with plastic is like adopting a stray dog*
> *— it might look a bit scruffy at first, but with a*
> *little love and glue, it'll bring joy to your life.*
> *Just don't expect it to sit still while you paint it."*

BOTTLE CAP MOSAICS

If you've ever looked at the growing pile of plastic bottle caps in your recycling bin and thought, *"These little things must be good for something"* — you're right. Bottle caps are the perfect size, shape, and colour to create **mosaics**: eye-catching designs you can hang on a wall, lean against a fence, or even use as tabletops. Instead of sending them to landfill, you'll give them a new, arty life.

What You'll Need

- A big collection of plastic bottle caps (different sizes and colours).
- A sturdy backing board (plywood, MDF, or even thick cardboard for a trial run).
- Strong glue (hot glue gun works best for speed, but any heavy-duty adhesive will do).
- Pencil and ruler (to sketch out your design).
- Optional: paint or markers to add details, clear varnish to seal your creation.

How to Do It

1. **Collect and Sort**
   Save caps from water bottles, milk jugs, fizzy drinks, juice cartons — basically anything. Sort them by colour and size into bowls or tubs. This is half the fun for kids, and it makes the design process easier later.
2. **Sketch Your Design**
   Decide on your mosaic pattern. It can be something simple — a rainbow, a flower, a smiley face — or ambitious, like a whole landscape or

superhero logo. Sketch it lightly onto your board with a pencil.

3. **Lay It Out**
   Before gluing, place your caps down to see how they'll look. Think of it like a plastic jigsaw puzzle. Adjust spacing and colours until you're happy.

4. **Glue Time**
   Stick each cap down one by one. Start from the middle of your design and work outward to keep it balanced. Press firmly so they hold.

5. **Finishing Touches**
   Once dry, you can paint the board background or seal the mosaic with clear varnish if you want to make it last longer outdoors. Indoors, it'll be fine as-is.

What to Make

- **Wall art:** Hang it in the kitchen or kids' room.
- **Garden decoration:** Lean it against a shed or fence for a pop of colour.
- **Tabletop:** Glue caps onto an old coffee table, then cover with a sheet of clear acrylic for a funky, upcycled look.

Why It's Brilliant

- Keeps loads of small, otherwise tricky-to-recycle plastics out of the bin.
- Teaches kids about reusing while sparking creativity.
- The results are bold, colourful, and guaranteed conversation starters.

Donny Wonder's Wonder Full Challenge:

> *"Try making a self-portrait out of bottle caps. Bonus points if people can actually tell it's you and not just a rainbow blob. If it looks more like a potato than a person, congrats — you've invented abstract eco-art!"*

MILK JUG HELMETS & MASKS

Who knew the humble plastic milk jug could double as headgear? With a little cutting and decorating, you can transform old jugs into **helmets, masks, or even full-on warrior gear**. It's the kind of recycling project that guarantees laughter, makes brilliant costumes, and proves that plastic doesn't always have to be rubbish.

What You'll Need

- Empty, clean plastic milk jugs (4-pint/2-litre ones work best).
- Scissors or a craft knife (grown-ups only for the tricky cutting).
- Elastic or string (to secure masks).
- Paints, markers, or stickers for decorating.
- Optional extras: aluminium foil, feathers, cardboard add-ons, googly eyes.

How to Do It

1. **Clean and Prep**
   Rinse the jug thoroughly (nobody wants a stinky helmet). Remove the label if you like, or keep it for a "brand-loyal knight" look.

2. **Decide Your Design**
   - o **Helmet:** Cut off the bottom of the jug. The handle becomes a nose guard or mohawk ridge, depending on how you wear it.
   - o **Mask:** Cut a flat panel from the side of the jug. Shape it into a face covering and cut out eye holes.
   - o **Crown or Tiara:** Slice the top off the jug, cut points into the rim, and paint it gold. Voilà, instant royalty.
3. **Cut Carefully**
   Adults should handle sharp scissors or knives. Round off edges so they're safe to wear. Try on your creation as you go to check the fit. (Warning: hilarity will ensue.)
4. **Add Fastenings**
   For masks, punch a hole in each side and tie string or elastic to hold it on. Helmets often just perch on the head — secure with a strap if needed.
5. **Decorate Wildly**
   Go mad with paints, stickers, or aluminium foil. Add cardboard horns, spikes, or wings. Feathers and googly eyes can turn a fierce warrior into something wonderfully ridiculous.

Ideas to Try

- **Medieval Knight Helmet:** Add a cardboard shield and pretend you're off to battle dragons (or the recycling bin).
- **Superhero Mask:** Colour it in bold shades, cut out a dramatic shape, and strike a heroic pose.

- **Space Explorer Helmet:** Paint it silver, stick on a straw "antenna," and pretend you're ready to land on Planet Eco.
- **Animal Mask:** Cut ears from cardboard, glue them on, and paint whiskers, stripes, or spots.

Why It's Brilliant

- Turns something boring and throwaway into hours of fun.
- Perfect for rainy days, school projects, or fancy dress.
- Costs next to nothing — you're literally making costumes out of the recycling.
- Sparks imagination while sneaking in an eco-lesson.

Donny Wonder's Wonder Full Challenge:

> *"Host a family milk-jug battle. Everyone makes a helmet or mask, then struts around like you're at a recycled fashion show. Bonus points if you keep a straight face. Extra bonus if the dog agrees to wear one too."*

PLASTIC BOTTLE LANTERNS

Plastic bottles are everywhere, but with a little imagination (and some fairy lights), they can be turned into **lanterns** that brighten up any room, garden, or campsite. They're simple to make, fun to decorate, and look amazing when they glow at night.

What You'll Need

- Clean plastic bottles (any size — water, soda, juice bottles all work).
- Scissors or craft knife (grown-ups only for the cutting).
- Battery-powered tea lights or LED fairy lights (never real candles — melted plastic is not a good look).
- Paints, markers, or tissue paper for decorating.
- Glue or Mod Podge if you're using tissue paper.
- String or wire if you want to hang them.

How to Make Them

1. **Clean and Prep**
   Remove labels, wash out the bottles, and let them dry. Clear bottles are best for a glowing effect, but coloured ones can look great too.
2. **Cutting Options**
   - **Classic Lantern:** Cut the top off a bottle and place an LED tea light inside.
   - **Hanging Lantern:** Cut a doorway near the bottom to slide in lights, then use the bottle's neck and a loop of string to hang it.
   - **Strip Lantern:** Slice the sides of the bottle into long vertical strips, then bend them outward like petals. Pop a light inside, and you've got a glowing flower.
3. **Decorate**
   - Paint the outside with bold designs — stars, swirls, or cartoon faces.

o   Wrap the bottle in tissue paper and glue it down for a stained-glass effect.

o   Use permanent markers for fine details.

4. **Light It Up**

Place your LED light inside, switch it on, and enjoy the glow. Cluster a few lanterns together for maximum effect.

Ideas to Try

- **Fairy Garden Lights:** Make mini lanterns with small bottles and hide them around plants.
- **Halloween Pumpkins:** Paint bottles orange, cut jagged "faces," and pop a tea light inside.
- **Camping Lanterns:** Use a 2-litre bottle, decorate it, and hang it in a tent or on a tree branch.
- **Party Glow:** String several bottles together with fairy lights inside each one.

Why It's Brilliant

- Turns boring bottles into something magical.
- Adds atmosphere to gardens, sleepovers, and parties.
- Safe for kids to make and use (as long as you stick to LEDs).
- Gives bottles a second life before they head to the recycling bin.

Donny Wonder's Wonder Full Challenge:

*"Make a lantern shaped like a famous landmark —
Eiffel Tower, Big Ben, or even your local bus stop.
Then switch it on and see if the neighbours recognise it.
Bonus points if it ends up looking nothing like what you
planned but still gets a 'wow'."*

WONDER FULL CRAFT CHALLENGES

If you've still got a pile of bottles, caps, and cartons staring at you, don't bin them yet. Here are a few silly, speedy, and surprisingly fun mini-projects that prove recycling can be more than sensible — it can be daft, creative, and wonderfully pointless in the best way.

1. THE PLASTIC CROWN CHALLENGE

Take the top half of a bottle, cut zig-zags around the edge, and decorate it with stickers, tin foil, or bottle caps. Place it on your head and declare yourself **King or Queen of Recycling**.

*"Finally, a crown you don't need a royal budget for.
Warning: does not grant actual power over your siblings."*

2. THE CUTLERY ORCHESTRA

Turn old plastic forks and spoons into a band. Tape them to a cereal box, pluck them like guitar strings, and perform a concert for your pets.

> *"If your dog looks unimpressed, that's just jealousy.*
> *Plastic rock stars are the future."*

3. THE MYSTERY MASK RACE

Give each family member a milk jug and five minutes. No rules, no instructions — just cut, stick, and decorate. When the timer ends, parade your creations. Bonus points if they look nothing like faces.

> *"You know it's gone well if Grandma ends up*
> *looking like a cross between*
> *Batman and a watering can."*

4. THE CAP TOWER SHOWDOWN

Stack bottle caps into the tallest tower possible without glue. Winner gets bragging rights, loser has to rebuild everyone else's tower when it falls.

> *"Physics meets recycling meets chaos. Guaranteed to end in either triumph or a very colourful avalanche."*

5. THE PLASTIC FASHION CATWALK

Make wearable "fashion" out of old bags, bottles, and wrappers. Strut through the living room like you're on a Milan runway. Extra points for adding bottle-cap earrings or crisp-packet ties.

> *"If someone doesn't shout 'What ARE you wearing?!' you're not doing it right."*

WHY DO THESE CHALLENGES?

Because recycling isn't just about bins and boxes. It's about looking at rubbish and realising it can spark creativity, silliness, and joy. You'll laugh, you'll make a mess, and you'll never look at a milk jug the same way again.

CHAPTER 13
GREEN GARDEN PROJECTS

Recycling indoors is fun, but the garden is where plastic really gets to show off its second life. Instead of heading for the bin, bottles, tubs, and odd bits can be transformed into tools that help you grow food, decorate your space, or scare the life out of the local pigeons.

In this chapter, you'll learn how to build a **mini greenhouse out of bottles**, craft **DIY plant pots** for seedlings, and even rig up **drip irrigation systems** to water your veggies while you put your feet up. And for a final bit of outdoor silliness, you'll create a **scarecrow made of odds and ends** — complete with a Donny Wonder hat, because even recycled guardians of the garden need style.

These projects aren't just fun — they're practical. They give plastic a second chance at usefulness, help cut costs in the garden, and make the outdoors brighter and greener (literally).

"Why buy fancy garden gear when your recycling bin is already full of it? Bottles don't just hold lemonade — they can build castles, water tomatoes, and terrify crows. Now that's multitasking."

BOTTLE-BUILT GREENHOUSES

Why throw bottles away when you can build something that grows life instead of clutter? With enough empty bottles, a bit of patience, and some garden enthusiasm, you can create a **mini greenhouse** (or even a full-sized one) that keeps seedlings warm, shelters plants, and makes your garden look like a mad scientist's eco-lab.

Option 1: The Mini Bottle Greenhouse

Perfect for kids, balconies, or just experimenting.

What you'll need:

- 1 large clear plastic bottle (2-litre soda bottle or 4-pint milk jug).
- Scissors or craft knife (grown-ups only).
- Soil and seeds/seedlings.

How to make it:

1. Cut the bottom off the bottle.
2. Plant your seedling in a pot or straight in the ground.
3. Pop the bottle over it like a cloche (a mini dome). The bottle traps heat and moisture, creating a cosy environment.
4. Unscrew the cap now and then to let it breathe and avoid mould.

Voilà — a greenhouse for one plant!

> *"It's basically central heating for your lettuce.*
> *And cheaper than running the boiler."*

Option 2: The Wall of Bottles

Great for bigger gardens or school projects.

What you'll need:

- Dozens (or hundreds) of bottles, all the same size (2-litre soda bottles are ideal).
- Wooden frame (like a shed frame or sturdy posts).
- Scissors, string or wire, and determination.

How to make it:

1. Cut the bottoms off the bottles.
2. Stack the bottles neck-to-base, creating long tubes. Thread a stick, cane, or wire through the middle to keep them aligned.
3. Build several of these "bottle columns."
4. Attach the columns side by side to a wooden frame, like making see-through plastic walls.
5. Once finished, you'll have bottle walls that trap heat and light just like glass — but at zero cost.

Option 3: The Full Greenhouse

Yes, people have actually built full-sized greenhouses out of thousands of bottles. It's a community-level project that looks incredible and works brilliantly. Check online for photos — they're part art installation, part vegetable factory.

Why It Works

Plastic bottles are clear, tough, and trap heat. That makes them perfect for greenhouse walls, acting just like glass but without the hefty price tag. They also divert mountains of bottles from landfill, which is a win-win.

Why It's Brilliant

- Gives bottles a brand-new life.
- Perfect science project for schools or families.
- Costs next to nothing (except your fizzy drink habit).
- Actually works — plants inside grow faster and stronger.

Donny Wonder's Wonder Full Challenge:

"See if you can build the world's tiniest greenhouse — just one bottle and a single pea plant. Or the world's silliest — a giant greenhouse shaped like a teapot. If the neighbours aren't confused, you haven't gone big enough."

DIY PLANT POTS

Before you rush to the garden centre to buy plastic pots (yep, more plastic!), take a peek in your recycling bin. Yogurt tubs, bottles, food containers — they're all potential homes for seedlings. With a bit of cutting, painting, and imagination, you can turn everyday rubbish into **planters that are cheap, cheerful, and surprisingly stylish.**

What You'll Need

- Any plastic containers (yoghurt pots, margarine tubs, ice cream tubs, juice cartons, soda bottles).
- Scissors or craft knife (grown-ups only).
- Nail, skewer, or screwdriver to poke drainage holes.
- Soil, seeds, or plants.
- Optional: paint, markers, stickers, washi tape for decoration.

How to Make Them

1. **Choose Your Container**
   Small yoghurt pots? Perfect for herbs or starting seeds.
   Big ice cream tubs? Great for salad leaves or flowers.
   Bottles? Slice them in half for instant planters.
2. **Add Drainage**
   Plants hate soggy bottoms. Poke a few holes in the base so excess water can escape. Put a tray or saucer underneath to catch drips if indoors.

3. **Fill and Plant**
   Add soil, then sow seeds or transplant seedlings. Water lightly to settle them in.
4. **Decorate (Optional but Fun)**
   - o   Paint the outside with bright colours.
   - o   Draw silly faces so your basil looks like it has hair.
   - o   Wrap in fabric scraps or old newspaper for a rustic look.
5. **Enjoy Your Upcycled Garden**
   Line your pots up on a windowsill, balcony, or patio. You've just saved money *and* kept plastic out of landfill.

Ideas to Try

- **Bottle Bottom Planters:** Cut the bottom off a 2-litre bottle, flip it upside down, and you've got a simple planter.
- **Hanging Planters:** Punch two holes near the rim of a bottle or tub, thread string, and hang them from a fence or balcony rail.
- **Carton Planters:** Juice and milk cartons can be cut in half and used like troughs — perfect for rows of herbs.
- **Funny Face Pots:** Draw faces on yoghurt pots, plant grass or cress, and watch it grow into "hair." Kids love giving their pots haircuts.

Why It's Brilliant

- Saves money on buying new pots.
- Perfect for small-space gardening.
- A fun way to involve kids in planting.

- Every container rescued from the bin is one less piece of waste.

Donny Wonder's Wonder Full Challenge:

> *"Make the weirdest planter possible. Could be a bottle with a moustache, a yoghurt pot spaceship, or a milk carton shaped like a dinosaur. Extra points if the neighbours stop to ask, 'What on earth is THAT growing on your windowsill?'"*

Drip Irrigation from Bottles

Tired of thirsty plants wilting when you forget to water them? Enter the humble plastic bottle — transformed into a **drip irrigation system** that delivers water slowly and steadily, right where your plants need it. It's cheap, clever, and makes you look like a gardening genius.

What You'll Need

- Plastic bottles (500ml for pots, 1–2 litre for garden beds, 5-litre for big thirsty plants).
- Scissors or craft knife.
- A pin, nail, or screwdriver (to poke holes).
- Soil and plants that need watering.

How to Make It

Option 1: The Upside-Down Bottle

1. Poke 2–3 tiny holes in the cap of the bottle with a pin or nail.

2. Fill the bottle with water.
3. Screw the cap back on.
4. Bury the neck of the bottle into the soil near the plant, upside down.
5. The water will drip slowly out, keeping the soil moist for days.

Option 2: The Sideways Soaker

1. Lay a bottle on its side.
2. Poke a line of tiny holes along one edge.
3. Bury it just under the soil, holes facing the roots.
4. Fill with water, cap it, and let it trickle gently along the row of plants.

Option 3: The Hanging Dripper (for pots)

1. Cut a small hole in the bottom of a bottle.
2. Hang it upside down over a pot with string.
3. Let it drip into the soil below. Perfect for hanging baskets or balcony plants.

Why It's Brilliant

- Saves water by giving plants just what they need, not floods.
- Keeps plants alive when you forget to water (or sneak off camping for the weekend).
- Costs nothing — it's recycling and irrigation in one.
- Great science experiment for kids: they can watch how fast (or slow) water seeps out.

Ideas to Try

- Add liquid fertiliser to the water bottle for a DIY "plant energy drink."
- Use clear bottles so you can see the water level dropping.
- Make a whole row of bottles in a veggie patch for stress-free watering.

Donny Wonder's Wonder Full Challenge:

"Set up drip bottles and then time how long they last. Bet on which one empties first. Loser has to serenade the tomatoes with a watering can guitar. Winner? They get bragging rights as Chief Lazy Gardener."

A SCARECROW MADE OF ODDS & ENDS (WITH A DONNY WONDER HAT)

Every garden needs a guardian. Not the serious, stone-faced kind — the scrappy, colourful, cobbled-together type that looks like it's wandered straight out of a Donny Wonder daydream. A scarecrow built from recycled odds and ends is part sculpture, part fashion disaster, and part eco-statement. And yes, it absolutely needs a hat worthy of Donny himself.

What You'll Need

- Old clothes (shirts, trousers, dresses, odd socks — the sillier, the better).

- A stick frame (two sticks tied in a cross, or even a mop handle).
- Stuffing (plastic bags, old newspapers, bubble wrap — great way to reuse what you've got).
- Gloves, boots, or shoes.
- String, cable ties, or twine to hold it all together.
- A hat (see below for the "Donny Wonder Hat" upgrade).
- Optional extras: sunglasses, masks, bottle caps for buttons, CDs for shiny eyes.

How to Make It

1. **Build the Frame**
   Tie two sticks in a cross. Plant the long one into the ground so it stands tall. This is your scarecrow skeleton.
2. **Add the Body**
   Dress the frame in old clothes. Stuff them with crumpled plastic bags, shredded cardboard, or old fabric scraps until they look pleasantly plump.
3. **Create the Head**
   Options:
   - A stuffed pillowcase tied at the neck.
   - A big plastic bottle or tub painted with a goofy face.
   - An upturned bucket decorated with bottle-cap eyes.
   - Draw or stick on features — the wonkier, the better. Crows are easily spooked by eccentric fashion.
4. **Accessorise**
   Add gloves for hands, boots at the base, and maybe a belt or scarf. Old CDs tied to the arms can

dangle and catch the sun, adding to the scare factor.

5. **The Donny Wonder Hat**

   No scarecrow is complete without a hat. Grab a battered old wide-brimmed hat, or make one from a plastic bucket, bottle base, or even an upturned salad bowl. Add flair:

   - Bottle-cap badges.
   - A feather from a milk jug mask project.
   - A sticker that says "Official Garden Guardian."

     This is the hat that seals the deal — and gives your scarecrow Donny Wonder levels of charisma.

Why It's Brilliant

- Uses up all kinds of plastic odds and ends.
- Protects your veg patch from hungry birds.
- Makes your garden look delightfully eccentric.
- Turns recycling into an art form.

Donny Wonder's Wonder Full Challenge:

> *"Give your scarecrow a name and a backstory.*
> *Is it Captain Bottle-Belly, defender of the cucumbers?*
> *Or Lady Poly Ethylene, guardian of the beans?*
> *Bonus points if you write them a theme tune*
> *and perform it while planting tomatoes."*

CHAPTER 14
THE BIG PLASTIC FINALE

We've come a long way together. From the miraculous invention of plastic to its creeping invasion into oceans, animals, and even our own bodies. From global bans and wild mushroom science to crafty bottle-cap mosaics and scarecrows in floppy hats. Along the way, we've laughed, built, swapped, and dared — all while tackling one of the biggest challenges of our time.

Here's the truth: plastics *are* useful. They've given us medical miracles, space exploration, and lightweight gear that makes daily life easier. But that same durability — the very thing that made plastic miraculous — is also what makes it dangerous. Once it's out there, it doesn't just disappear.

We can't fix everything at once. None of us can. But we *can* do something. Every swap, every craft, every refill jar or plastic-free weekend adds up. And when millions of people each do a little something, the impact is massive.

So as we close this book, here are Donny Wonder's final (yeah right, final, haha!) words of encouragement:

> *"The world is one big campsite, and it's our job to keep it clean and thriving. Leave it better than you found it, share your snacks, and never let the rubbish pile higher than the tent."*

PLASTICS: USEFUL BUT DANGEROUS

Let's be fair to plastic for a moment. It really did change the world. It gave us lightweight car parts, affordable packaging, waterproof jackets, life-saving medical equipment, even space suits. Without it, half the modern conveniences we take for granted would still be luxuries.

Plastic's superpower has always been its **durability**. It doesn't rot, rust, or crumble away like wood or metal. A plastic bottle can hold fizzy drink today and still be sitting in a ditch 500 years from now. That's both genius... and a disaster.

Because what started as a miracle quickly became a menace. The very qualities that made plastic so helpful — cheap, flexible, indestructible — are the same ones that now haunt us. Mountains of bottles, bags, and wrappers that never break down. Microplastics sneaking into water, food, and air. Animals mistaking rubbish for dinner. And us, discovering tiny plastic hitchhikers in our blood and lungs.

It's not that plastic is evil. It's that we used it without thinking. We built a throwaway culture around a material designed to last forever. That's like inventing indestructible plates and then deciding they should only be used once at a picnic.

> *"Plastic is like that friend who helps you move house but then won't leave your sofa for six months. Brilliant at first, a nightmare later."*

The recap is simple: plastics are powerful, practical, and often essential. But they're also dangerous if left unchecked. Which means the challenge for us is not to banish plastic from our lives completely, but to use it wisely — and stop treating it like disposable rubbish when it's anything but.

WE CAN'T DO EVERYTHING, BUT WE CAN DO SOMETHING

When you step back and look at the plastic problem, it feels enormous. Oceans clogged with bottles. Rivers carrying tonnes of rubbish to the sea every day. Invisible fibres floating in the air and lodging in our lungs. And with plastic production still climbing, the mountain seems to grow faster than we can dig at it.

It's tempting to shrug and say, *"Well, what difference can I make?"* After all, you're just one person, one family, one household. You're not running a recycling plant or writing global laws. But here's the truth: **change never starts with doing everything — it starts with doing something.**

WHY SMALL ACTIONS MATTER

- **Ripple effect:** When you make a swap (say, bringing your own coffee cup), other people notice. Suddenly, the person in line behind you wonders if they should try it too. Small choices spread like ripples on a pond.
- **Collective power:** One family cutting out plastic bags saves a handful each week. Multiply that by

millions of families, and suddenly billions fewer bags end up in the ocean.

- **Signals to businesses:** When shoppers start demanding plastic-free packaging or supporting refill shops, companies notice. Consumer choices drive corporate change.
- **Building habits:** Once you start with one swap, it becomes second nature. That makes the next swap easier. Before you know it, you've chipped away at half your household's single-use plastics.

PICK YOUR BATTLES

You don't need to fight every plastic villain at once. Focus on what makes sense for you:

- If you're a parent packing lunches, start with reusable containers and refillable bottles.
- If you're a fashion fan, try buying fewer polyester clothes or washing them in a microfibre bag.
- If you're into crafts, channel your waste into mosaics, lanterns, or milk-jug helmets.
- If you're a gardener, set up bottle irrigation or start seedlings in yoghurt pots.

Find the swaps and habits that fit your life, and leave the rest for now.

WHAT YOU CAN'T CONTROL

It's okay to admit there are limits. You can't personally stop companies churning out plastic packaging. You can't clean up every river. You can't reverse the tonnes of microplastics already in the air. But you *can* control your corner of the campsite — your home, your habits, and your choices. That's not nothing. That's huge.

THE BIGGER PICTURE

Every environmental win has started small. Smoking bans, recycling systems, even seatbelt laws — they all began with a handful of people saying, *"This is silly, let's change it."* Plastic is no different. The more of us who "do something," the louder the message becomes, until governments and businesses are forced to act on the big scale.

> *"You can't fight every battle. But if you pick up one piece of rubbish on the beach, use one bamboo toothbrush, or shout BINGO after one plastic swap, you're already part of the fight. Imagine if everyone did just that — the campsite would look a whole lot tidier."*

*

The point is simple: we can't do everything. None of us can. But we can all do *something*. And that "something" is how big changes begin.

CLOSING WORDS OF ENCOURAGEMENT

So here we are — the end of the plastic trail. We've dug through history, peered at microplastics under the microscope, laughed at daft crafts, and even built scarecrows in floppy hats. And after all that, the lesson isn't complicated: **the world is one big campsite, and it's our job to keep it clean and thriving.**

Think about it. On a campsite, everyone shares the same space. You wouldn't leave your rubbish piled up in the middle of the field, because the next campers would have to deal with it. You'd tidy up, pack it out, and maybe even leave a little firewood stacked for whoever comes next.

Earth works the same way. We don't own it outright — we're just borrowing our pitch for a while. Our kids, their kids, and all the creatures sharing the space with us deserve a site that's fresh, safe, and still full of wonder.

We can't promise spotless tents or glitter-free grass, but we can all make sure the rubbish doesn't pile higher than the campfire.

We can leave the world better than we found it!

*"Take only memories, leave only footprints...
and maybe a bottle-cap mosaic nailed
to the fence for the next lot to admire.
The campsite's big enough for everyone
— let's keep it clean, thriving,
and full of stories worth telling."*

Illustrated and packed with 99 creative, wacky, and wildly fun indoor activities, this book is your go-to guide for turning drizzle into dazzle. Whether you're 5, 10, or just a grown-up kid at heart, there's something here to spark every kind of mind—makers, movers, puzzlers, snackers, storytellers, and daydreamers alike.

Here's what's waiting inside:

Chapter 1: Crazy Crafts Corner – Get gluey, glittery, and gloriously creative

Chapter 2: Boredom Busters: Games & Giggles – Rain won't stop this fun-fest of indoor games

Chapter 3: Brilliant Brain Teasers – Puzzles, riddles, and noodle-twisting challenges

Chapter 4: Indoor Energy Adventures – Burn off energy with wild weather-proof activities

Chapter 5: Mini Makers Lab: Easy Experiments – Safe and silly science to blow your socks off

Chapter 6: Imagination Station – Puppet shows, dress-up, and creative chaos encouraged

Chapter 7: Snack Attack! – Easy-peasy recipes and snackable experiments

Chapter 8: Quiet Time Creations – Calm crafts and chill-out fun to soothe stormy afternoons

Chapter 9: Make-Believe Missions – Dream up characters, adventures, and worlds of your own

Story Sparks – Imagination Igniters – 20 magical story starters to inspire your next great tale

And there's more! Don't miss the special "Mix, Match, and Make It Wonder Full!" bonus chapter for limitless creative combinations, Challenge Trackers to chart your rainy-day victories, and the super-fun Create Your Own Wonder Badge section—perfect for celebrating your newly crowned indoor-activity champions!

PLUS: Keep an eye out for Donny Wonder Dares and Wonder Tips sprinkled throughout—little bursts of silliness and inspiration to surprise and delight.

For Parents, Caregivers, and Educators:

This book isn't just about filling time—it's about unlocking creativity, encouraging independent play, and turning rainy-day frustrations into joyful discovery. All 99 activities are screen-free, low-prep, and designed to work with what you already have at home.

Perfect for:

- Home use on rainy days or weekends
- After-school or holiday boredom busters
- Classrooms, clubs, or rainy-day childcare
- Grandparents, babysitters, or travel kits

Whether your child is a bundle of boundless energy, a quiet thinker, or somewhere in between, there's something here that will engage, entertain, and inspire.

RAIN OR SHINE, THIS BOOK PUTS THE POWER OF PLAY RIGHT INTO THEIR HANDS—AND PEACE OF MIND INTO YOURS.

INDOOR RAINY DAY ACTIVITIES FOR KIDS OF ALL AGES

99 Fun, Creative, and Screen-Free Things for Children to Do at Home - including Games, Crafts, and Storytelling!

Available in paperback and hardcover from all good bookshops, and also from Amazon as an eBook.

From laugh-out-loud classics like Capture the Flag and Tug of War, to splash-tastic water games like Water Balloon Dodgeball and Sprinkler Limbo, this book is bursting with 100 exciting outdoor activities perfect for kids aged 9 to 12.

But wait—there's more!

You'll also discover glow-in-the-dark night games, backyard Olympics challenges, nature-inspired creativity, and even a Backyard Science Lab where you can make erupting volcanoes, solar ovens, and balloon-powered race cars!

**250 HILARIOUS, GROSS, AND
WILDLY IMAGINATIVE QUESTIONS!**

GET READY TO LAUGH, SQUIRM, AND THINK WAY OUTSIDE THE CEREAL BOX!

Donny Wonder's **Would You Rather?** is a gut-busting, brain-bending activity book packed with 250 of the silliest, strangest, and most side-splitting questions ever imagined. Perfect for kids aged 7-12, this book is ideal for road trips, rainy days, classroom chaos, sleepovers, family game night, and anywhere that needs a little more weird.

Each themed chapter explodes
with imaginative dilemmas:

Wonderfully Weird
Bizarre brain-ticklers and topsy-turvy logic
Food Fiascos
Deliciously disgusting and edible absurdities
Creature Features
Mythical beasts, talking animals, and questionable pets
School Shenanigans
Detention-worthy decisions and backpack blunders
Outdoor Adventures
From jelly-mountain hikes to trampoline forests
Rainy Day Dilemmas
Couch-bound chaos and stormy silliness
Silly Superpowers
Unusual abilities you didn't know you needed
Gross but Great
Farts, slime, toe jam... and that's just the beginning
Donny's Daily Disasters
Straight from the mind (and diary) of Donny Wonder
The Bonkers-Fueled Final Showdown!
The wildest chapter of all

Would you rather have a backpack that sings lullabies or toes that squirt ketchup?

Would you rather burp glitter or sneeze spaghetti hoops?

Why kids (and grown-ups) love this book:

Screen-free fun for creative minds
Perfect icebreaker for classrooms and parties
Great gift for birthdays, holidays, or road trip survival
Encourages imagination, laughter, and silly debates

Whether you're playing alone, with friends, or in front of a confused llama, this book guarantees giggles, groans, and gallons of...

"WHAT WOULD YOU EVEN DO?!"

MORE FROM

WONDER FULL BOOKS

*A Wonderfully Weird Would You Rather!?! Book
for Kids Ages 7–12 and Probably Teens*

*Indoor Rainy Day Activities
for Kids and Teens (Illustrated)*

*Summer Activities for Kids 9-12 (Illustrated)
100 Fun Outdoor Games for Boys and Girls*

Printed in Dunstable, United Kingdom

68877877R00080